THE FUTURIST OPTION

The

Futurist

Option

by
Carl E. Braaten
and
Robert W. Jenson

NEWMAN PRESS
New York/Paramus/Toronto

Library of Congress
Catalog Card Number: 73-127792

Published by Newman Press
Editorial Office: 304 W. 58th St., N.Y., N.Y. 10019
Business Office: Paramus, New Jersey 07652

Printed and bound in the
United States of America

Contents

PART III

IMAGING THE FUTURE

Introduction

Karl Barth and Rudolf Bultmann exchanged letters toward the close of Barth's career. In his letter, Barth compared the two of them to a whale and an elephant, each keeping his eye on the other: the one squirting a torrential stream of water into the air, the other trumpeting earthquaking sounds through his trunk. They can see and hear each other down by the oceanside, but neither understands a word the other is saying. Like the whale and the elephant, Barth and Bultmann have been speaking in different tongues.

The question we have today is: "Were they really so different?" They lived through the same shattering events, spoke the same language, came from the same Church background, studied at the same schools, learned the same theologies, and faced the same critical issues in thought and life. To be sure, they veered away from each other. As theology became polarized, Barth became the leader of the conservatives who wanted the restoration of the tradition, and Bultmann became the sponsor of the liberals in quest of new interpretations. But such differences are always possible within the same broad horizon of concern and framework of thought. In the next generation these differences began to fade away and the underlying bond of unity showed more clearly. Many of us discovered sooner or later that we could not chart our future by following only the compass readings of either Barth or Bultmann. When one faces the prospect of shipwreck, it doesn't really matter whether one strikes the reefs on the starboard or the port side. The reefs are history itself, and eschatology is the compass. Any theology that would go beyond Barth and Bultmann will have to map out a new way to understand eschatology and history.

The concept of the future is the hermeneutical key to a new understanding. In Christianity there is an interest in the future that cannot be surrendered, because the promises by which it lives in history throw it forward in hope toward the awaited fulfillment. The God of promise, the God of hope, the God of history—he is the God and Father of our Lord Jesus Christ.

1

Barth and Bultmann rediscovered part of this: Barth called God "the Eternal Future," and Bultmann called him "the Insecurity of the Future." Faith, they agreed, is "openness to the future," and Christianity "altogether eschatology." But the enchantment of the past lingered by way of idealism and its offspring, existentialism. God was seen as the Power after future, but this future was defined as the *eternal* future, not a time with its own narratable content, but the crisis of every time, equidistant to all times. Hope was given no specifiable object: we were called to hope to keep on hoping. Of this future and this God and this hope there was therefore nothing to *say*—the dialectical theology came to no gospel. And although Barth later developed a mighty formulation of content, it may be that he did so only by hiddenly giving up the original eschatological insight.

The gospel is, after all, a *story*. As a word of the future it is not, therefore, properly a mere command: "Be open." It is a promise with narrative content. The questions we must insistently ask are: "What does the gospel promise?" and "How does the gospel promise it?"

If the following essays belong together in one volume, it is because they share a complex of motifs. All take seriously the common-sense apprehension of life's temporality: that we have past, present and future. All suppose that the Christian gospel enforces this attitude. All think that the gospel communicates the reality of all three arrows of time, but that it is by opening the specific reality of the future that the gospel grants also the past and the present. All are therefore concerned to become clear about the reality especially of the future, and about the use of future language in our proclamation and self-understanding. And all express, explicitly or implicitly, the opinion that this particular clarity is, at least for now, the exigent clarity for the life and mission of the Church. Or one may put the concern as follows: Having "rediscovered" the biblical eschatology, what are we going to do with it, other than explain it away or use "eschatology" as a euphemism for something else?

These accents link this volume with the theological initiatives of Wolfhart Pannenberg and Jürgen Moltmann. However, it is not our intention to offer a discussion of their theological systems or to provide a commentary on what we might be doing that is different. Nor do we make predictions about how long "theologies of hope" may remain fashionable. Perhaps not long, since the affirmations that we wish to make are not novelties. If God is once identified as the One who raised Jesus, or if he is seriously said to "justify" the "ungodly," all our matter is already stated. What we want to do is take affirmations which have always been at the heart of the gospel, and hammer them against their traditional theological mitigations until they begin to make more theological difference than they have done. And we do indeed claim that this task is the current task of theology, and predict that either theology will persevere in it or the renewal of the Church will fail.

One of the special concerns that runs through the chapters of this book is to demonstrate that orientation toward the future is the ground for the freedom to take the present seriously. The futurist option that we develop here is not to be mistaken for a futurism that flees from the burdens and joys of the present. It is not an escapist trick; it is not creating a new "god of the gaps" so that we merely slip into the future the problems we cannot solve in the present. If anything, it calls us to the front line of world history as the missionary people of God. The logic of prepositions and tenses is inescapable for us all, and we trust no one dreams of subverting it: we live *in* the present, *in view of* the past, *in face of* the future. It would be a miraculous breach of tautology indeed to live otherwise than now; it would be equally remarkable to live otherwise than before the future. These are not options; the options are *how* our present rhymes with the future it faces and the past which is laid upon it.

Indeed, there are finally only two options: do we now—indeed and of course *now*—live as persistence in the past or as acceptance of the future? Is our God the Immutability of the past or the Uncontrollability of the future? A volume on the futurist option is one that wants to untangle these two options, vote for the second as that affirmed by the gospel, and see how it works out in some few areas of reflection.

There is one particular misunderstanding of the so-called "theology of hope" that must be corrected. The theology of the future allegedly places the word of promise in sheer antithesis to all past and present reality. There is no doubt that Jürgen Moltmann's use of the technical formula *inadaequatio rei et intellectus* in his *Theology of Hope* has given rise to this misunderstanding. A strict interpretation of this formula might suggest that what we hope from the future is in total contradiction with what we know of the past or experience in the present. The reality (*res*) does not correspond to the knowledge (*intellectus*). Only the future reality, only what does not yet exist, can correspond to the word of promise. But this formula is theologically inadequate.

The motif of contradiction is important in theology. It is implied whenever Christians pray, "Thy Kingdom Come." It is an axiom of the Reformation doctrine of justification—*justus in spe, peccator in re* (righteous in hope, but in actuality a sinner). It is not less the motivating impulse of a Christian revolutionary ethic, which draws on the power of negative thinking. On the other hand, the idea of a *total* antithesis between promise and reality is not tenable in Christian theology.

First, it would nullify faith in a *real presence* of the eschatological reality of God in the person of Jesus of Nazareth. Jesus of Nazareth is the one past-historical event to which the promise for the future of life has found its correspondence. The Word has become flesh. So too, all subsequent reality that is "in Christ" experiences the future of God already under the conditions of earthly existence.

Second, if the promise had positive relation only to the future and an exclusively negative relation to the past and present, theology would be driven into complete isolation. Theology, which reflects on the word of promise, would have to exist in pure contradiction to a philosophy that reflects on the phenomena of experience.

Third, theology would also be cut off from historical research, which inquires into the documents of the past. That is, historical research would not possess theological relevance since historical life would be thought to provide no provisional approximations (sacraments or sign-events) of that future to which the promises point.

Fourth, Christian political ethics would line up on the side of *total* revolution, if the expected future of promise necessarily arrives in opposition to all existing structures.

Fifth, the message of promise would set the Church against all the hopes and goals of the secular world, and the word of promise would be preached as a scourge of sheer judgment. For if the gospel announces a future that is totally against our human present, then it cannot be the good news of promise and fulfillment, but only bad news of doom and destruction. There must be continuity also between existing reality and the ultimate future if the end result of the history of promise is not to be the cancellation of the history of creation.

Resident in the dialectic of continuity and discontinuity is a possibly confusing terminological difference between the two authors of these essays, of which the readers should be aware. Braaten's entry into theology was by way of Tillich, Jenson's by way of Barth. These things leave their marks; one mark is variant use of "religion." Braaten uses the word to evoke the fundamental structure of self-transcendence which is the peculiar reality of man—for Braaten it is basically a good word. Jenson uses "religion" for the way in which, according to him, we in fact carry out our self-transcendence, as retreat into the past—for him it is basically a bad word. Clearly, a uniform terminology could be devised. But it would have been artificial for us to do so, for each of us wishes to retain for his own purpose the weight of the everyday reference and emotional freight of the word "religion": Braaten for access to the deep structure of human life, Jenson for polemic against unauthentic realizations of that structure. Perhaps this terminological stubbornness signals abiding material disagreement, but if so, we are not now able to say where it lies.

In Part II of this book we seek the horizon of the future in political ethics and the mission of the Church in the world. In Part III we seek new incorporations of the future in Christian life. The sensibility or imagination that functions within the framework of the Christian hope for the future dares to transform given realities and to open experience in the present to new meanings and hence to new reality. Christians who are open to the future of God want to hear and to see and to taste new things or to perceive old things in a new way. It is this openness to new things and to the future which has already taken shape in Jesus our Lord that binds together the political and liturgical, the ethical and the aesthetic, reflections in Parts II and III.

PART I

Futurizing the Hope

1

The New Theology
of the Future

Carl E. Braaten

This chapter is an attempt to trace the course of theology through
to its eschatological "new beginning" in the thought of Wolfhart
Pannenberg. In a previous essay, "Toward a Theology of Hope"
(published first in *Theology Today,* July, 1967, and then in *New
Theology* No. 5), I dealt with the thinking of Jürgen Moltmann
and Pannenberg together. That might have had the effect of
blurring their differences. Here I am interested in setting forth the
system of categories that is most vital in eschatological theology,
and therefore find it useful to focus mainly on Pannenberg's
thought. Placing this essay first has the added merit of acknowl-
edging the priority of Pannenberg's thought with respect to the
theme of the future.

I

THE PAN-ESCHATOLOGICAL DREAM

Karl Barth began and ended his theological career on an eschatological note. As the young theologian of crisis, eschatology
was his key word. He made the striking claim: "Christianity that
is not entirely and altogether eschatology has entirely and altogether nothing to do with Christ."[1] Toward the end of his long
journey in *Church Dogmatics,* he had second thoughts about wid-
ening the meaning of eschatology that it overlaps with everything that is essentially Christian. He raised a protest against
"the broadening of the concept of the eschatological which has

[1] Karl Barth, *The Epistle to the Romans,* tr. by Edwyn C. Koskyns (Oxford University Press, 1933), p. 314.

9

become so popular in the last decades."[2] It is obvious that he is thinking of the popularity of Bultmann and his school after World War II. In their language everything that has transcendent significance and is a matter of existential decision is spoken of as "eschatological." So Barth cried out: "The time has surely come when we should awaken from this pan-eschatological dream."[3]

There is a double irony in this appeal. First, in striking out against the Bultmannians, Barth is involved in a very belated self-criticism. He was the one who first dreamed the pan-eschatological dream. Secondly, Barth offers no concrete evidence that he himself ever managed to awaken from that dream. Barth began to see dimly the need for a new contouring of theology in which the eschatological dimension of hope and the orientation to the future would be given their due, and he intended to accomplish that in the fifth volume of his *Church Dogmatics*. But he never got around to writing it. The promise went unfulfilled. In his study of Barth's concept of eschatology, Tjarko Stadtland points this out and offers the soundest explanation: "For many it was painful that Barth declared that he no longer wished to write his eschatology (Vol. V, *Church Dogmatics*). But could he really do that from the starting point that was his?"[4]

From where we now stand in theology, Barth's starting point appears to be the same as Bultmann's—the transcendental Word of God as conceived within an eschatology of the eternal present. Eschatology was defined without focus on the future. The fact that Barth and Bultmann found themselves on opposite sides of so many debates in modern theology disguised—apparently both from themselves and their closest pupils—their underlying bond of unity. This unity becomes especially visible when the spotlight of eschatology is turned upon them. Wolfhart Pannenberg and Jürgen Moltmann called theology to an awakening when they challenged the legitimacy of an anti-eschatological eschatology.

[2] Karl Barth, *Church Dogmatics*, tr. by G. W. Bromiley (Charles Scribner's Sons, 1962), Vol. IV, 3, second half, p. 912.
[3] *Ibid.*
[4] Tjarko Stadtland, *Eschatologie und Geschichte in der Theologie des jungen Karl Barth* (Neukirchener Verlag des Erziehungsvereins, 1966), p. 189.

Eschatology without the future of the eschaton is no eschatology at all, but only axiology or mysticism. It is not the "broadening of the concept of the eschatological" which needs to be deplored, but rather the shift away from the category of hope in the oncoming future of God to the category of faith in his eternal presence. The movement in theology beyond Barth and Bultmann to the new theology of the future is an attempt to develop a more consistent eschatology (*konsequente Eschatologie*) in which the dimension of the future is not swallowed up by the eternal blitzing in from above. The term *konsequente Eschatologie* usually recalls the position of Albert Schweitzer and his school (Martin Werner and Fritz Buri). It means essentially that Schweitzer interpreted Jesus' ministry, all his words and acts, from a consistently eschatological perspective. By "eschatology" Schweitzer meant a strictly future coming of the kingdom of God, in line with the expectations of Jewish apocalypticism. This created a problem for theology, so keenly felt by Schweitzer himself. If Jesus expected the kingdom in his immediate future, then the fact that history has been running its course for two thousand years is proof positive that his hope did not happen.

The first Christians managed to retain formal continuity with Jesus' expectation by looking forward to a speedy return of Christ. But history itself has proved them wrong. This problem can be solved by converting the future object of expectation into a hidden but real dimension of the present. This is in effect what happened in the first centuries when Christianity underwent Hellenization. The eschatological gospel was defuturized into a mystical worldview. And although much of modern theology since Karl Barth has flattered itself for de-Hellenizing the gospel, at the crucial point it has not been able to make a clean break. Eschatology is deprived of the future by stressing the presence of the kingdom of God now. Barth defuturized eschatology by way of christology, Bultmann by way of anthropology.

In this chapter we shall be tracing the theme of the future in the thought of Wolfhart Pannenberg. It has become customary to view Moltmann as the chief representative of the theology of the future, with Pannenberg a somewhat loose associate. Not infrequently one finds watchers of German theology drive a wedge between their two ways of thinking. Moltmann's theology of hope is set over against Pannenberg's theology of history.[5] Our term —theology of the future—could embrace them both. For hope and history are interpreted in light of the eschatological future. However, I choose to confine my analysis to Pannenberg's thought, not merely to make my task easier, but to help rectify the misconception mentioned above. It was, in fact, Pannenberg who initiated the breakthrough to the new doctrine of the future. Already in 1959 Pannenberg began publishing articles in the leading journals which laid the foundations for his present position.[6] Then in 1961 Pannenberg edited a volume of essays, *Revelation as History*. A controversy was stirred up; critics pounced on the seemingly excessive claims of the new theology: revelation happens *as* history, not in a suprahistorical sphere; revelation speaks in the language of facts, not first in words of interpretation; historical research is able to penetrate to these facts; revelation can be grasped by reason; the resurrection of Jesus is an historical event, etc. These dazzling assertions were read as sheer antitheses to the prevailing certainties of theology. It was generally overlooked that these assertions were not anti-theses at all, but were syn-theses of a new kind, made possible by the reactivation of the future tense in eschatology. Pannenberg was setting forth an historical conception of revelation from the perspective of eschatology, and not on the old ground of positivistic historicism. Pannenberg's book was not merely about revelation and history, but about eschatology. Eschatology is the magnetic needle which orients the position of revelation and history in relation to each other. And the needle points to the pole of the future.

Moltmann published his *Theology of Hope* in 1964. It displays

[5] For instance, James M. Robinson, "Revelation as Word and as History," *Theology as History*, Vol. III of *New Frontiers in Theology*, ed. by James M. Robinson and John B. Cobb, Jr. (Harper & Row, 1967), p. 89.

[6] The futurist perspective appeared in the following essays by Pannenberg, beginning in 1959 with the publication of "Heilsgeschehen und Geschichte," and then in succession "Kerygma und Geschichte" (1961), "Die Krise des Schriftprinzips" (1963), "Was ist eine dogmatische Aussage?" (1962), "Was ist Wahrheit?" (1962); "Einsicht und Glaube" (1963), "Analogie und Doxologie" (1963); "Hermeneutik und Universalgeschichte" (1963). All these essays appear in a collection entitled *Grundfragen systematischer Theologie* (Göttingen: Vandenhoek und Ruprecht, 1967).

the full force of the category of the future. In one unfortunate section Moltmann strained to distinguish the path he was taking from Pannenberg's. He stressed those points at which he could show significant divergence, while playing down the fact that the theme of the future was pulling them in the same direction. If that was not clear as a fact to Moltmann then, at least now he freely acknowledges that "today I find more agreement than difference in the later writings of Pannenberg."[7] What holds them together, in spite of many differences, is their common acceptance of the ontological priority of the future, their theory of knowledge which aims to reveal what reality lacks, that is, the role of the principle of negativity in showing up the proleptic structure of language and events, as well as their firm adherence to the history of Jesus as revelation of God. The key to this complex of ideas is that more "consistent eschatology" which places the light of the future of God and his kingdom upon our understanding of man and his world.

II

ESCHATOLOGY AND CHRISTOLOGY

The theology of the future arose while the new quest of the historical Jesus was in full swing. We would fail to understand its deepest motive if we read it as something else than as an attempt to interpret the history of Jesus of Nazareth. An historically focused interpretation must deal with the issues of apocalypticism, its future orientation, the resurrection event, and how these together constitute the conditions under which it is meaningful to speak of God's self-revelation in Jesus.

Apocalypticism

The preaching of Jesus and the Easter kerygma about him arose within the context of Jewish apocalyptic thought. Jesus' message was eschatological from the inside out; he shared the

[7] J. Moltmann, "Antwort auf die Kritik der Theologie der Hoffnung," *Diskussion über die "Theologie der Hoffnung,"* ed. by Wolf-Dieter Marsch (Chr. Kaiser Verlag, 1967), p. 222, n. 9.

apocalyptic hope of Judaism for the future coming of God's kingdom. Christology cannot ignore this fact. However, that is not to say that Jesus and the early Church merely continued the Jewish hope intact. Rather, that hope underwent a double conversion. First, it was modified by Jesus' own message and ministry; secondly, it was reshaped by the early Church's preaching of the crucified and risen Jesus. Eschatology comes filtered through the cross and resurrection events from that point on.

Pannenberg's insistence on the importance of Jewish apocalypticism for christological thought does not stem from any natural fondness on his part for its odd ways of thinking, especially when we consider its elements of determinism, fatalism, dualism, otherworldliness, and its esoteric numerologies. Rather it is his intention to grasp what is new and unique about Jesus of Nazareth against the background of his actual historical situation, one decisive factor of which was the tradition of Jewish apocalypticism. And when we take into account the New Testament as a whole, the marks of Jewish apocalypticism are conspicuously evident. The whole of reality is historicized from the beginning of creation to the very end. The cosmos itself is drawn into the process of history that leads to a future consummation. If eschatology is not linked to the horizon of universal history, it gets bogged down in the tribal history of a special people or the existential history of a private person. The historifying of the world in apocalypticism is thus the original cradle of Pannenberg's idea of a universal history, however post-Hegelian its conceptual form. Indeed, the modern idea of the historicity of man and the rise of the historical consciousness in the West have their ultimate roots in the biblical vision of all reality as history. If apocalypticism is renounced lock, stock and barrel, as in existentialist demythologizing, it is difficult to see how we could even retain continuity with Israel's belief in the One God. For the idea of One God implies that he is the ultimate power over all things. The anti-divine forces in history will be vanquished in the future as God establishes his rule throughout the creation. The basic Christian symbols of judgment, resurrection, new creation, the salvation of mankind, and the kingdom of God are all projected as anticipations of the future within the horizon of late-Jewish apocalypticism. There is thus too much at stake for the

Christian system of belief to overlook the meaning of apocalyptic thought.

Futurity

Jesus' ministry was an anticipation of the future of God's kingdom. But it had proleptic character in that Jesus took something that was still future into his present. This is what was distinctive about Jesus in contrast to apocalypticism: "Jesus underscored the *present impact* of the imminent future."[8] Pannenberg does not view Jesus as an apocalyptic visionary, contrary to certain unfounded allegations.[9] He follows the interpretation of Ulrich Wilckens who defines the historical problem as one of understanding Jesus "in the context of Jewish apocalypticism without making him an apocalyptist."[10] In their view Jesus proclaimed the kingdom of God as an imminent reality with such exclusiveness and urgency that the decision for the kingdom is bound up with a person's relation to Jesus himself. It is not so much the content of Jesus' message that was new, but rather the attachment of the kingdom's advent to his own person. God himself was drawing so near in Jesus' announcement of the kingdom that the early Church could view Jesus' earthly ministry as the dawning of the kingdom already, as a pre-actualization of the ultimate future. Hence, it is not wrong for New Testament theology to stress the *presence* of the kingdom in Jesus' ministry. But what is really present? It is the *future* of the kingdom already arriving. The element of futurity must not be dissolved into a present-tense eschatology.

There are schools of New Testament interpretation which opt for either the *presence* or the *future* of the kingdom (C. H. Dodd versus A. Schweitzer) in Jesus' teaching. By critical means the

---

[8] W. Pannenberg, *Theology and the Kingdom of God* (The Westminster Press, 1969), p. 53. Pannenberg stresses the real differences between Jesus and apocalypticism most clearly in his book, *Jesus—God and Man* (The Westminster Press, 1968).

[9] E.g., Hans Dieter Betz, "On the Problem of the Religio-Historical Understanding of Apocalypticism," in *Journal for Theology and the Church*, ed. by Robert W. Funk (Herder & Herder, 1969), p. 194.

[10] Ulrich Wilckens, in his review of August Strobel's book, *Die apokalyptische Sendung Jesu*, appearing in *Theologische Literaturzeitung*, LXXXIX (1964), p. 671.

attempt is made to eliminate the opposing group of passages as inauthentic, or to put a forced reading on them. Pannenberg finds the uniqueness of Jesus' message precisely in the juxtaposition of the opposing sayings.[11] His idea of prolepsis is the key to understand how the future can be present without thereby ceasing to be future. There is no realized eschatology in the sense that the future passes over into the present, leaving everything to the memory and nothing for the imagination of hope. In Jesus' ministry the future of God's rule becomes a presently active power, yielding glimmerings of his final *doxa*. The present appearance of the kingdom in Jesus is grounded in the power of the future; ultimately and ontologically the present is derived from the future.

By allocating such priority to the future in Jesus' teaching it is evident that Pannenberg will arouse some static from some of the more established schools of interpretation. Existentialist demythologizing is plainly wrong in dismissing futurity "as a hangover from Jewish apocalytpic."[12] And the scheme of *Heilsgeschichte,* as presented by Oscar Cullmann, is equally wrong in thinking "that Jesus understood the kingdom of God as beginning in his presence and has only to be fufilled in the future."[13] Pannenberg's proposal is a more radical one; it involves an ontological reversal of the relation between present and future. Our conventional habit of connecting the future to the present as an additional track that runs on ahead is not an adequate model in grasping Jesus' eschatological outlook. Therefore, if we try to think in a new way, by giving to the future its priority, we may have struck upon a hermeneutically more fruitful path, and at the same time lay hold of a new approach to some of the knottiest philosophical problems in regard to knowledge, language, historical existence, and ultimate reality.

Resurrection

Pannenberg is trying to give systematic expression to the his-

[11] W. Pannenberg, "Appearance as the Arrival of the Future," *New Theology No. 5,* ed. by Martin E. Marty and Dean G. Peerman (The Macmillan Company, 1968), pp. 118-19.
[12] W. Pannenberg, *Theology and the Kingdom of God,* p. 54.
[13] *Ibid.*

torical fact that the entire early Christian faith—its doctrine and cult, its kerygma and mission—presupposed the resurrection of Jesus. Even the throwback to the pre-Easter Jesus and the tendencies that guided the various transmitters of the gospel traditions bore the marks of Easter faith. The resurrection of Jesus is the gateway to the theology of the future. There is no Christian hope for the future that is not based on the unique event of Jesus' resurrection.

What is the meaning of the resurrection? It is God's vindication, says Pannenberg, of Jesus' claim that the decision of his hearers in relation to the kingdom is bound up with their attitude to his person. The authority of Jesus is based upon the authenticity of his claim. If the kingdom he preached would not have arrived or would have brought no fulfillment of any kind, his personal claim in relation to the kingdom of God would have been nullified. But there was fulfillment; his resurrection meant new life. The resurrection of all the dead, or at least of all believers, had been expected. Instead, only a preliminary fulfillment was reached in the resurrection of the one man—Jesus of Nazareth. This event would not be confined to Jesus, since he is called "the first-born from the dead" (Col. 1:18). The future would bring the universal fulfillment. Therefore, believers can live toward the future in hope, confident that what God has done already to Jesus of Nazareth will ultimately happen to them. On account of the resurrection we can speak of the eschatological future becoming present in Jesus. There is a real presence of the absolute future in the particular event of Jesus Christ; for the world as a whole the future remains open; the final salvation of mankind is an object of active hope and prayerful anticipation.

The resurrection is pivotal for the doctrine of revelation. Only with the arrival of the eschaton in Jesus does God reveal himself in a final way. Jesus can be called the final self-revelation of God on the condition that the final future of all reality has arrived in him. This is what it means to speak of Jesus Christ as eschatological occurrence. If a person examines the resurrection reports and reaches a negative verdict, this could well represent the loss of belief in God's self-revelation. So Pannenberg claims that the result of this examination "is absolutely fundamental to Christian faith."[14] He is echoing the apostle Paul's statement, "If Christ has not been raised, then our preaching is in vain and your faith is in vain" (1 Cor. 5:14). It is at this juncture that Pannenberg asserts that the resurrection accounts in the New Testament can pass the test of historical reason. This appeal to reason has brought him much notoriety. There is no little tragedy in the fact that when Pannenberg and Moltmann have tried to explain their conviction about the resurrection to some American audiences, they are ready with a name for it—fundamentalism. The liberal establishment in American theology has handed belief in the resurrection of Jesus over to the fundamentalists, and the latter have turned it into a miracle story about a freakish physical fact. Even a casual reading of Pannenberg would convince a person that his rational arguments are not nourished by the biblicism or supernaturalism of American fundamentalism.

The skepticism that frequently greets Pannenberg's thesis about the verifiability of the resurrection carries no great weight in itself. It is understandable as a prejudice arising out of a widespread dogmatism that asserts *a priori* that the resurrection is both historically impossible and existentially meaningless. But this skepticism can be challenged at two levels, first concerning the nature of historical reality, and second concerning the method of historical research. Suffice it to say here that Pannenberg's affirmation of the resurrection occurs in conjunction with a concept of historical reality and knowledge that breaks open the closed system of positivistic historicism, with its talk about *bruta facta*. The accusation that Pannenberg is "turning back the clock" by reviving the historicism of the nineteenth century is usually set forth on the basis of the existentialist idea of history. The existentialist idea of history is a retreat into subjectivism; it thinks of itself as the antithesis to the objectifying view of positivistic historicism, as though no new third alternative could possibly arise. Since existentialism failed to break through to a new concept of historical reality, it has had enormous difficulty in speaking about the meaning and goal of world history.

I think the point is this: if Pannenberg is maintaining the his-

---

[14] W. Pannenberg, "Focal Essay: The Revelation of God in Jesus of Nazareth," *Theology as History*, p. 125.

torical verifiability of the resurrection of Jesus, the magnitude
of that claim must be measured within the horizon of *his* understanding of historical reality and historical reason. For he pat-
ently is not claiming that the historicity and meaning of the resurrection of Jesus can be asserted on any old view of history. The
broader questions of the ontology of history and historiology are
involved as much in the denial as in the affirmation of the historicity of Jesus' resurrection. These questions cannot be suppressed
in the interest of sheltering Easter faith in a theologically pa-
trolled DMZ. The future of the faith stands or falls with the future
of Christ which God himself secured by putting death behind him
forever. To believe anything less than this would be to abandon
any meaningful criterion of what counts as Christian faith. Faith
cannot be based on faith; faith must have its objective ground in
reality beyond itself.

III
THE PROLEPTIC STRUCTURE OF REALITY

Hermeneutics

Theology reaches universal dimensions in Pannenberg's theology.
The One God of Israel can be spoken of adequately only in relation to the whole of reality. This calls for the recovery of the
motifs of the universality, wholeness, and unity of all reality in connection with the idea of God. Therefore, theology must become a
universal science. Its positivistic confinement to a special revelation as well as its exclusive reliance on biblical exegesis and the
dogmatic tradition needs to be overcome. Such a restriction en-
dangers the monotheistic idea of God whose claim to Lordship is
universal. But if theology is a universal science, then what is usually called philosophy is already included within the scope of theology. For there can hardly be two universal sciences side by side.
Their statements about the world, man, and history would inevitably come into conflict.[15] Pannenberg brings to mind the classical view of the Alexandrian fathers who thought of theology quite

---

[15] W. Pannenberg, "The Crisis of the Scripture-Principle in Protestant
Theology," *Dialog,* Vol. 2 (Autumn, 1963), p. 308.

simply as the true philosophy. Or perhaps Pannenberg could say with Paul Tillich that philosophy becomes theonomous when its quest for ultimate truth and reality unites with the biblical revelation of the One God.

Pannenberg uses philosophical arguments to make way for the theological assertion that the eschatological reality of God appeared in the history of Jesus. He acknowledges that his philosophical reflections are carried out on Christian presuppositions. But does that necessarily count as a strike against them? The presuppositions themselves are not used as arguments, but only enter into the psychological matrix of inquiry.[16] The eschatological character of the Christ-event has implications for our understanding of the world, man, and history. On the other hand, the internal problems of philosophy—epistemological and ontological—may be shown to bear within them a kind of "logic of anticipation" in relation to eschatological theology.

To speak of God in connection with the totality of reality is to speak of him historically and eschatologically; historically, because history is the most comprehensive horizon of reality, and eschatologically, because history is incomplete. It can be thought of as a whole only by way of an anticipation of its future end. The idea of God must be thought of, then, in relation to the openness of man and his world toward the future. The self-revelation of God in Jesus of Nazareth is an event which reveals and constitutes history as a whole, by entering into history as its future and final end. If the idea of universal history is a theme of theology, so far as it speaks of the God of history and his eschatological revelation in Jesus' resurrection, so also is it an essential theme of the hermeneutics of history in general.[17] Historical and theological hermeneutics meet at the problem of universal history. Theology takes up this theme when it speaks of God in Christ as the meaning and goal of all history. Historical study anticipates it when dealing with the meaning of particular events. For the meaning of a single event can be had only in relation to its context, and the meaning of the context can be understood in turn only in relation

[16] W. Pannenberg, "Über historische und theologische Hermeneutik," *Grundfragen systematischer Theologie*, p. 152.
[17] *Ibid.*, p. 140.

to a still larger context, until the idea of universal history is reached.

The idea of the inescapability of universal history is developed by Pannenberg in relation to the inner problematic of modern hermeneutics, as that becomes evident in the thought of Wilhelm Dilthey and Martin Heidegger. Dilthey applied to the study of history the basic hermeneutical axiom that in any text the meaning of the parts is related to the whole, and vice versa. Accordingly, the significance of any historical event is related to history as a whole, i.e., universal history. The category of meaning in history is thus bound up with the problem of its totality. Since, however, history has not yet come to an end, but is open to the future, the idea of its wholeness can only be constructed backward from its anticipated end. History can be thought of as a whole only in light of its finality. Thus the meaning of any of its single events, as well as of its broader contexts and movements, breaks open the question of an eschatological future. An aporia is reached: no historian stands at the end of history; yet one has to be presupposed to understand the meaning of any part of it. The assertion that the end of history has occurred proleptically in Jesus of Nazareth thus becomes the indispensable key for the interpretation of history.

Anticipation

Heidegger followed up Dilthey's insight, only he restricted it to individual human existence. His analysis of the historicity of existence is made in abstraction from the question of the unity, wholeness, and end of history. Instead, he speaks of the possibility of man grasping his existence as a whole by anticipating its future end. In this way Heidegger broke through to the idea of the existential-ontological priority of the future, and the primacy of the category of anticipation. Pannenberg accepts both of these ideas, but frees them from Heidegger's attempt to grasp the whole of existence, its meaning, and all its possibilities, from the future of its absolute end in death. A crucial existential problem is thus posed: human existence acquires its meaning only by anticipating its end, but if the only end to be anticipated is death, how can its retroactive effect on life fail to threaten every positive sense of meaning? For his part Pannenberg does not accept death as the ultimate limit projected by the anticipative consciousness of man. Rather, it belongs to the proleptic structure of human existence to inquire beyond all limits, even the limit of death itself.

The idea of the proleptic structure of human existence is an important link in Pannenberg's argument. Basically it means self-transcendence. An analysis of this tendency in man helps to illuminate what it means to speak of God. The idea of self-transcendence is expressed in modern anthropology by the term "openness to the world" (*Weltoffenheit*).[18] Man inquires beyond himself, beyond the limits of his present situation, through his anticipations, wishes and hopes. In the process of questioning man strikes out into the realm of the unknown, beyond every answer that has already been reached. But is the process of continual questioning meaningful in itself? Hardly! The meaning of man's questioning presupposes that an answer can be reached. The myth of Sisyphus, the one condemned by the gods to roll a stone up a hill all his days with no hope of reaching the top, is an intolerable picture of man's situation. The idea that there is no hope of reaching the top, no anticipation of reaching an answer to the question implied in existence, would lead to nihilistic doubt. Then not only the answers but also the process of questioning itself is undermined. "Creative inquiry is always expecting an answer. It is meaningful to make an inquiry only so long as an answer is regarded as possible."[19]

Man is one who not only asks questions about this or that. He himself is the core of the question he poses. His existential questioning reaches out beyond himself and his world. Does it reach into a void? Is there anything there at the end of his reach? This question, however, may be based on a wrong assumption. It assumes that the question man asks about himself is posed apart from and prior to all contact with the reality after which he seeks. Pannenberg calls that an "abstraction." "The question is always framed through the involvement with the reality in question."[20] This means that the answer cannot be derived from the question;

[18] W. Pannenberg, "The Question of God," *Interpretation*, XXI, No. 3 (July, 1967), pp. 289ff.

[19] *Ibid.*, p. 304.

[20] *Ibid.*, pp. 307-08.

instead, an outline of the answer is dimly sketched only in response to the impact of the answer. The mistake of natural theology, with its great proofs of the existence of God, is to confuse the relation between question and answer. These are not proofs of the existence of God so much as they are descriptions of the question-structure of human existence. They reveal man reaching beyond himself and his world toward that which infinitely transcends both. Pannenberg is here endorsing Tillich's handling of the classical arguments for the existence of God. In the sequence of the argument it is possible to conclude from the question to the answer because some awareness of the answer is implied in the question. In other words we could say that religious experience is the *prius* of philosophical reflection about the ultimate question of human existence and its possible answer.

Man's experience of himself as a question drives him into the open future. Both Pannenberg and Moltmann trace our historical experience of reality to its religious roots in Israel's experience of the freedom and faithfulness of the God of history. This is also the basis of the modern notion of the "historicity of existence," that is, the freedom to be open to new events which have not yet occurred. This takes us full circle. The form of the question has been shaped by a religious answer. But will this religious answer work in the future? Moltmann has defined the problem this way: "The point is not so much the origin of the modern historical consciousness, but rather its future."[21] Can the question of human existence be answered by directing it back to its originating ground in history? If it is the nature of the question-structure of human existence to go beyond every answer that has already been attained, then will not the biblical revelation of God be overtaken and outstripped by new questions?

It seems to be the modern experience of man that his questions drive him into the open future where his questions far outdistance any of the answers that can be found in the historical tradition. It is in face of this modern attitude of radical inquiry that the quest for God can be understood and answered only by rediscovering the eschatological future as a divine mode of being. Only if

[21] J. Moltmann, *Theology of Hope* (Harper & Row, 1967), p. 82.

God's nature is futural can he be the answer to the undying quest of human existence that proceeds beyond every present. Our conception of God can be outstripped by the questioning process without rendering the biblical revelation of God obsolete, "because this God in his almighty freedom is no concrete being, but the Lord of the future toward whose coming the world is moving. . . . As the answer he does not put an end to the human quest but has freed it to proceed in openness. In this way Christian language of God proves its worth in terms of the openness of human existence to go beyond every limit. This openness is disclosed in its depths by this language, and for this reason then refers back to the God of the Bible as its ultimate, unsurpassable fulfillment."[22]

Traditional theism has not been able to withstand the onslaughts of radical questioning, Pannenberg believes, precisely because in its formulation the notion of the futurity of God and his kingdom was prevented by the Greek idea of the eternity of God as a timeless presence without change.

Truth

The historical experience of reality as future-directed also affects the concept of truth.[23] The Western concept of truth can be traced back to two roots, the Greek and the Hebrew. For the Hebrews, in contrast to the Greeks, truth is reality seen as history. Truth is not something that lies hidden in the core of things, but something that happens. Pannenberg does not exaggerate the differences between the Greek and Hebrew ways of thinking. They have some aspects in common; for example, both think of truth as something dependable and lasting, and opposed to surface appearances. And although the Hebraic view of truth is oriented to historical change and an open future, trust in God is based on his trustworthiness which has already been shown in his historical action. This is not totally unlike the Greek confidence in the rational structure of the cosmos, whose dependability has been already experienced in the past. Nevertheless, the difference remains. The Greeks could not bring together truth and change.

---

[22] W. Pannenberg, "The Question of God," *op. cit.*, p. 314.
[23] Cf., W. Pannenberg, "Was ist Wahrheit?" *Grundfragen systematischer Theologie*, pp. 202ff.

The unity and wholeness of truth could only be grasped in terms of a concept of reality whose essence is unchangeableness, and therefore without beginning and end. The biblical concept of truth, in contrast, required and created change. Truth is not what is and always has been; truth is what will be. The unity of truth has to be grasped as history. Historical change is not something that lies on the level of appearance and opinion, where the Greeks left it. Instead, historical change can be taken up into the concept of truth, if truth itself has a history.

Already these terms hint that Pannenberg is nearing the vicinity of Hegel's concept of reality and truth. For Hegel "the true is the whole."[24] The truth of the whole, or the whole truth, becomes visible only at the end. Pannenberg sees that this Hegelian thesis makes contact with the biblical view of truth in two respects. First of all, truth is not thought of as something timeless and immutable. It is bound up with the process of history in which changes occur. Secondly, the process of history, so full of contradictions along the way, is seen as a unity in light of the end, and the real significance of any event is judged in terms of the final outcome. To be sure, Hegel himself lost the horizon of the future in his philosophy, since he identified his own point of view with the end of history.[25] He had no genuine eschatology. Without it he could not solve the problem of how to maintain the unity and wholeness of history so long as the end of history had not yet arrived. So he caused it to arrive in his own philosophy, a bit too prematurely for most people.

The proleptic character of the Christ-event thus makes possible a conception of truth which overcomes the contradiction in Hegel's thought. The unity of truth can be held, together with its historicity and its openness to the future, because the end of history has appeared in Jesus of Nazareth without ceasing to be future. The lack of this perception in Hegel's philosophy had other consequences; the contingency of historical events, the uniqueness of the individual, the historicity of reason, etc., were all slighted.[26]

---

[24] *Ibid.*, p. 218.
[25] *Ibid.*, p. 219.
[26] W. Pannenberg, "Glaube und Vernunft," *Grundfragen systematischer Theologie*, p. 247.

The widely felt need for an historical view of reason and the experience of historical relativism can be positively understood on the basis of the eschatological structure of God's revelation in history.

IV

THE ONTOLOGICAL PRIORITY OF THE FUTURE

Philosophy

Finally, we shall draw out further implications from the idea of the ontological priority of the future. One of the classical problems of philosophy has been the relation between reality and appearance, or between essence and existence. In the Parmenidean-Platonic line, reality was understood as the appearing of something that always is. This left no room for the idea of the future, and, accordingly, no weight was given to the contingency of particular events. Pannenberg sees that there was always another line in Greek philosophy, the Socratic motif in Plato's thought. In the Socratic idea of striving for the good, the element of futurity was implied, insofar as one can only strive for what one does *not yet* have, but hopes to attain. This Socratic line was further extended by Aristotle in his theory of motion, insofar as the good is identified with the goal of movement. In this way Aristotle gave an ontological foundation to a futuristic element. However, Aristotle crippled this idea in two ways. First, the goal of movement was made to indwell things as their *entelechy*. Hence, things only become what they already are in germ. Secondly, Aristotle said that the goal of the movement must exist somewhere, else it could not serve as the cause of motion, the final cause. But if the goal already exists within reality as potentiality, then the result of the movement is to bring forth nothing really new. Thus, the Parmenidean line also finally prevailed in Aristotle, as it had done in Plato. Nevertheless, Pannenberg sees in classical philosophy the roots of another line, which can view "appearance as the arrival of the future," instead of as "the unveiling of timeless being."[27]

²⁷ W. Pannenberg, "Appearance as the Arrival of the Future," *New Theology No. 5*, pp. 112ff.

This view makes room for contingent events, for the famous "accidental truths of history" which have always been Christianity's chief liabilities in face of the Parmenidean notion of being and truth. This philosophical ontology, joined with the mythological reversion to primal time (*Urzeit*) and its archetypes, has stood in the way of an ontology of the future. Christian theology, contrary to its innermost nature, has often preferred timeless universals, absolute principles, and eternal orders. A true evaluation of contingency, newness, freedom, change, the individual, and time itself, has been retarded by the power of an ontology whose spirit is alien to these aspects of experience and reality.

The Idea of God

Pannenberg believes that there lies in Jesus' message of God and his imminent kingdom the undeveloped potential for a new ontology. Of course, Jesus did not work out a new idea of God in systematic terms. Yet, in his preaching the very being of God is so fused with his coming kingdom, that one cannot be thought without the other. The future of God's lordship and sovereign rule is fundamental in his being as God.[28] Until now Christian theology has not drawn out the implications of the priority of the eschatogical future in Jesus' message for its doctrine of God and of creation. We are now living in a new intellectual situation which demands rethinking the idea of God with futurity as his original mode of being. For one thing, the atheistic criticism of the traditional idea of God, which was forged on the anvil of Greek philosophy, with its timeless being and eternal cosmos, cannot be brushed aside as of no consequence. This criticism is valid so far as its target is the idea of God as an objectively existing being, the single most perfect being among all beings (*Ens perfectissimum*). For another thing, the futurity of God is intrinsically appropriate to release new meanings from Jesus' proclamation of the rule of God for a more adequate interpretation of nature and history, individual and community.

To define God as the power of his rule, on the basis of Jesus'

---

[28] W. Pannenberg, "The God of Hope," *Cross Currents* (Summer, 1968), Vol. XVIII, No. 3.

message, leads to the idea of God as the "power of the future."[29] In his very being God is the future of the world. He is the common future and unifying force of all contingent events in nature and history. Man's experience of the future is ambiguous; he looks ahead with anxiety or hope. This experience of the ambiguity of the future is connected with the real contingency of events. They do not have to happen as they do. A deterministic model is not an adequate explanation of events. The contingent events may be thought of as chance happenings, as erratic occurrences. Or they may be thought of as personal acts that spring meaningfully from the power of the future. This is possible if through the events there appears a self-identical unity that connects them in a meaningful way. Contingency and unity are preconditions for thinking of the future as personal power.

To think of the future as prior to the past and the present is, at first, an exercise that threatens hernia of the mind. Our commonest habit is to think of the priority of the past. The future is then only an empty space which gets filled in as events unroll according to laws written into the nature of things. It might be thought, therefore, that to reverse this way of thinking leads to two mistakes, the neglect of the past and the dismissal of God to the future. That would flatter our pride; it would mean we could "play God" in the present. The present itself would be, then, a mere empty space to be filled by the choices of our "dreadful freedom." This is an existentialist view of time which Pannenberg is far from sharing.

Creation

The future that is effective in the present is the future of every event and epoch of the past. The continuity of past and present is created by their common future horizon. The contingent events that are the objects of memory are linked to the future which is now for us the object of hope. Every past event was created out of the power of the future which will create every future finite event. Here Pannenberg is working out a new doctrine of creation, interpreting it more with reference to the eschatological future

[29] In my book, *The Future of God* (Harper & Row, 1969), I have developed this basically new image of God in the form of a "little dogmatic."

than to the mythological past. As the future of every past and the very present, God is near to both as their creative origin, their revealer of meaning, and their ultimate goal. God is not to be thought of as a timeless immanence in a changeless cosmos, but rather as the creative eschaton of reality in process. Pannenberg takes one further step along this line. As the power of the future God does not only appear to be future in relation to the past and present. For it has been argued that his futurity is grounded not in himself, but in the temporal structure of human experience. However, if God is not his own future, there would be some other future beyond him, and this would have to be thought of as God. The very idea of God requires that we think of him as the ultimate future. The direct implication of this is that God must be thought of as "pure freedom."[30] To be wholly free is to have one's future already within oneself. It could be said that man has his future in God, and therefore finds his fullest freedom in radical dependence on him.

There are innumerable implications which follow from the futurist option in theology. In this book we will be pursuing them in our own way. In the next essay we will examine various radical theologies to test the hypothesis whether the loss of the eschatological horizon may not be the root of that atheism which is cropping up on Christian soil. The "death of God" may be the sort of change theologians are getting back on their de-eschatologized (i.e., defuturized) currency. Then we will explore the theological significance of Ernst Bloch's reactivation of the theme of the future in philosophy. In still other chapters we will convert the element of futurity into an asset that pays off intellectually as well as ethically and aesthetically. When the deepest strivings of mankind are brought into correlation with the biblical revelation of God as the coming Lord, the imagination is liberated to achieve new perceptions and the will is mobilized to take new strides toward freedom.

---

[30] W. Pannenberg, *Theology and the Kingdom of God*, p. 63.

2

The "Death of God" as Futureless Theology

Carl E. Braaten

This essay was prepared as a lecture for a German audience, given first at a conference of Lutheran pastors in Berlin and next to students of theology at the University of Mainz. A somewhat briefer version of it was published under the title "Radikale Theologie in Amerika," in *Lutherische Monatshefte,* February, 1968. I have here given it a new title to display my thesis that theology was making a casket for God when it tried to take the future out of eschatology. If we speak of God apart from the future, then we are paving the way to speak of the future apart from God. The result is the atheistic consciousness which has made its appearance in theology and the Church. The answer, I think, lies in the direction of healing the breach in the unity of God and the reality of the future.

I

BIRTH PANGS OF THE FUTURE

In a prophetic way Eugen Rosenstock-Huessy made a statement that is being proved true by the "death of God" movement in theology: "When people consider God as having been our maker in the past only, and abandon eschatology and a belief in God's future, their belief in God's presence disappears too. So Nietzsche, finding a Christianity devoid of faith in Last Things, rightly shouted, 'God is dead'."[1] The "death of God" wing of radical theology is today rattling the bones of a theological skel-

[1] Eugen Rosenstock-Huessy, *The Christian Future* (Charles Scribner's Sons, 1946; Harper Torchbook edition, 1966), p. 97.

eton that had already lost its eschatological life. The God who is declared dead is the God of the past, not the God of hope, who holds our future in his power. The "death of God" movement has been analyzed from many angles. Our analysis proceeds from an interest in eschatology. The "God is dead" theology should be seen as the end-result of an already de-eschatologized Christianity. To say that God is dead may be only a different way of describing a theism in which eschatology had died. That is to say, a God without his future leads to a God without hope; and a God without hope leads to a hope without God. And a hope without God eventually withers away into hope-lessness and future-less existence. For God is the ground of our hope as the power of the future. A non-eschatological theism is a deadly thing; it is hopeless. If there ever were a god who fit such an ism, he would be better dead than alive.

Unless we are smugly satisfied with the status quo in theology, we ought to listen to the most radical voices in our midst. Everything can be seen as a symptom of something, even when it is not confused with a state of health. What does it mean to call for Christian faith and theology to go on without reference to the reality of the living God? Not only extremists are saying that the time and place in which we live is characterized by the feeling of God's absence. So strong is the feeling of his absence that only an extreme verdict can grasp the truth of this situation: he must be dead. Hence, the "death of God" thinkers are involved in the unprecedented experiment whether it is possible to be Christians without belief in the living God. If this is a-theism, it is not exactly the same kind of atheism with which theology has already been familiar. It is not an atheism that is pursued passionately for its own sake. Rather, it appears more as a side effect of integrating contemporary experience into the Christian faith. For the sake of this integration the "God-hypothesis" must be removed. The claim is being made by some that neither the gospel nor the twentieth-century believer sustains a serious loss of power and meaning when the name of God is dropped as an empty and meaningless noise.

The reactions from the theological establishment have been severe and swift to quash the revolt of the radicals. Most of these reactions are clearly justified. They have been able to point out the glaring weaknesses. For example, it has been noted that van Buren has lapsed back into logical positivism, with its crude use of the empiricistic verification principle, and he has misappropriated Hare's idea of the blik. Hamilton is also vulnerable; he can give no good reason why he singles out Jesus from among the world's saints and sages as the unequaled model for a modern man's style of life. As for Altizer, he has composed an arbitrary canon of inspired writings from Hegel, Blake, and Nietzsche in place of Paul, Luke, and John, and indulges in language so visionary as to be utterly divorced from empirical facts and concrete experiences. There is no doubt that an impressive case can be, and already has been, made against each of the new radicals from the point of view of traditional patterns of thought. And when serious arguments fail, one can resort to the stale jokes scribbled on bathroom walls.

One redeeming feature of the new discussion about God, no doubt, is the humor that runs throughout. If one happens to believe in God at all, he cannot help but hear echoes of the laughter of God intermingling with his own most serious thought about God. Yet, there is need for caution. It is a common failing among theologians to devise tactics to dismiss what they do not wish to hear, especially when they have reached middle-age. Instead, we should ask, is there any positive meaning in the "death of God" phenomenon for the future of theology? It has happened before that Church theology succeeds to its own interior disgrace to drown out the prophetic voices of radicals like Strauss, Feuerbach, Nietzsche, Marx, and Freud, only to be required later to pay a heavy penalty for having turned a deaf ear to what was being said *when* it was being said. The penalty is loss of interior integrity and credibility. Then theology appears to be the last refuge of those who resist change, a sort of ideological comforter for those whose destinies are closely tied up with the sagging fortunes of obsolete institutions. What I am saying is that the mere rejection or refutation of "death of God" radicalism is of no importance whatsoever; indeed, it could be dangerous, unless it is done for the right reasons. Good reasons are not enough. They may be only buying time for our traditional ways of doing theology. They may prevent us from sighting the new conditions which the radical theologians rightly say must be met if theology is to have a future. These new conditions are the important thing. It may well be that the "God" who is dead is but a name that functions for conditions of religious experience and doctrinal belief that are crumbling in the modern world. It may be that the pain and travail which theology is now undergoing are the birth pangs of the future. The blunt and brutal word that "God is dead" may be heard as a way of shaking off the dead hand of the past, so far as it prevents theology from being obedient in the present to the new conditions now being born. It was Henri de Lubac, one of the first of the new progressives in Roman Catholic theology, who keenly observed, "Everytime that mankind abandons a system of thought, it thinks it is losing God."[2] How common for the people of God to try to encase him in their most cherished traditions of piety and belief. How frequently loyalty to tradition has cancelled the invitation to welcome new things which God is pouring into our present from the abundance of his gracious future.

The zeal for newness and openness to new conditions in our modern life must be regarded as an asset. Also the demand to be secular and to make our theology indigenously American must not be flippantly dismissed as of no value. Altizer has pointed out that first William Blake and then Hegel envisaged America as the place where a revolutionary future would occur. From Hegel's lectures on the philosophy of history he quotes: "America is the land of the future: in it, in the time lying before us . . . the significance of world history will be revealed."[3] Now is the time for America to seize the opportunity to free itself from European guardianship and to accept its vocation of leadership in an industrial, secular and technological society. Van Buren, for example, states that a truly contemporary way of doing theology must be secular, and to be secular it must use the empirical, pragmatic,

---

[2] Quoted by J. B. Metz, "Zukunft gegen Jenseits?" in *Christentum und Marxismus-Heute,* ed. by Erich Kellner (Zürich, Europa Verlag, 1966), p. 223.

[3] Thomas J. J. Altizer, "Theology and the Contemporary Sensibility," *America and the Future of Theology,* ed. by William A. Beardslee (The Westminster Press, 1967), p. 25.

and linguistic methods of English-speaking culture. These methods, he feels, are most appropriate in a culture shaped by modern
science, technology, and industrialization.[4] I agree that any theology of the future will have to come to terms with these perva-
sive conditions in a way that no previous theology has ever done.
Van Buren's formulation of the theological task is attractive
and challenging: "How may a Christian who is himself a secular man understand the gospel in a secular way?"[5] The fact that
van Buren defines the gospel without its inherent eschatological
thrust and his neglect of the futuristic factor in the modern secular outlook need not detract from the cogency of his question.

The attempt of some American theologians to graft the existentialist categories of thought onto American experience will
be sloughed off by that experience itself. William Hamilton believes that he can detect a new mood of optimism sweeping
American culture, creating an uncongenial climate for the pessi-
misms of existentialism and neo-orthodoxy. The shift is from the
inner life and merely I-Thou relations to political action and the
communal sense of "We-ness." As Hamilton sees it, this is a self-
sufficient optimism, not "an optimism of grace, but a worldly optimism."[6] It is based upon a trust in the future of this world as
such. Whether this is a hidden way of affirming the reality of
God, whether such an attitude is not ultimately derived from a
faith in God who keeps man's future open and ignites hope even
in times of blackest despair and manifest earthly tragedy, is an
issue to which Hamilton has given no careful attention. A correlate of this future-oriented optimism is a rejection of the authority of the past. In overcoming the heteronomous use of the
past as authority, radical theology calls for a detachment from the
past as a requisite condition for the renewal of theology. At least
this goes for some of the radicals. Altizer says, "To a sophisticated European, America must appear as a desert, a desert shorn
of the vegetation of history. But a desert can also be a gateway

[4] Paul van Buren, *The Secular Meaning of the Gospel* (The Macmillan
Company, 1963), p. xiv.
[5] *Ibid.*, pp. 14, 17.
[6] William Hamilton, "The New Optimism—From Prufrock to Ringo,"
Radical Theology and the Death of God, co-authored with Thomas J. J.
Altizer (The Bobbs-Merrill Company, 1966), p. 169.

to the future."[7] And Hamilton says, "America is a place and a people without a past."[8] It used to be that when Americans acknowledged this to Europeans, it took the form of a humble confession. Now it is a matter of pride; there is no longer a trace of an inferiority complex. Verging on a new provincialism, they seem to be saying that American theology must disengage itself from European theology, for European theology always takes too many detours into the past to be alive to what is going on in the present. America inherited from Europe the self-image of theology as being at home in the university or the church. Theology was academic—it explained things; or theology was a function of the organized church, reflecting on inherited doctrine. Within the radical movement the conviction is voiced that theology must move "from the cloister to the world"[9] and thus at last fulfill the meaning of Luther's reformation. Theology is more like the brain trust of revolutionary action in the world. Its task is not so much to interpret the past as to be the probing instrument of revolutionary change. Altizer proclaims, "The radical Christian is a revolutionary," and "must not be thought of as a reformer."[10] The idea of reformation is a conservative one, and presupposes the primacy of the past. The idea of revolution presupposes, on the other hand, the primacy of the future. Harvey Cox, too, who is by no means a "death of God" radical, argues that although Christian theology must always be oriented to history, history is more than the sum of things past. History is happening in the present and the future is born through revolutionary change. A theology of history must thus be more akin to a "theology of politics" or a "theology of revolution."[11] The radicalism of Cox's theology is not marked by the cry that "God is dead" but instead that the proper horizon of theology is the present and future history of man. Its idiom is not limited to the private and personal sphere of religious experience but is forged instead in the con-

[7] Thomas Altizer, "America and the Future of Theology," *ibid.,* p. 17.
[8] William Hamilton, "Thursday's Child," *ibid.,* p. 87.
[9] William Hamilton, "The Death of God Theologies Today," *ibid.,* p. 36.
[10] Thomas Altizer, *The Gospel of Christian Atheism* (The Westminster Press, 1966), p. 26.
[11] Harvey Cox, *The Secular City* (The Macmillan Company, 1965), p. 107.

text of the forces at work in the secular city. Theologians who have been trained to look backward or inward for the stuff of their theology are understandably shaken by a reversal of method that drives theology forward and outward.

These conditions which one or another of the radical theologians cites as the *sine qua non* of theology in the future are methodically revolutionary. Many fear that they spell the death of theology altogether. I believe another interpretation is possible and preferable. In spite of its Olympian attitude to the Church, to its history, traditions and institutions, radical theology may be clearing the ground of a lot of rubbish that stands in the way of a new birth of theology. It may be that when theology is sore pressed, it will return to the missionary situation in which the people of God live from the essentials of hope toward the future of God's promised kingdom. Theology may repent of the loss of its original eschatological shape and dynamics. When one takes the claims of the radical theology literally, as so many critics have done, it seems quite easy to dispose of it as a lot of best-selling nonsense—nonsense also to that modern secular man whom all the radicals are courting. To be sure, the radicals are by no means in agreement about this man. Who is he? It is not unusual to hear them exclaiming of each other's portraits, "I wonder where he found *his* 'modern man'."[12] Nevertheless, I believe it more prudent to search out the positive meaning underlying radical theology. And so I say the theological cramps we are now experiencing, shared to some degree by all modern theologians, may be the birth-pangs of something new and better in theology, if only we can find the key to the storehouse of eschatological explosives in the history and person of Jesus of Nazareth. If this is impossible to do with integrity, we ought to admit defeat, and not carry on the pretense any longer of being Christians. My hope is that the incipient future-orientation of secular theology, its often inarticulate forward-looking movement, may give us useful leverage to make a fuller recovery of the eschatological ground and content of primitive Christian faith. This may then lead to a new the-

[12] See, for example, Paul van Buren, *The Secular Meaning of the Gospel*, p. 68, and Langdon Gilkey, "A New Linguistic Madness," *New Theology No. 2* (The Macmillan Company, 1965), p. 44.

ology in which the kingdom of God which broke from the future
into the life and history of Jesus finds a point of convergence
with the futuristic interests of modern man, however secular the
terms in which the hopes for the future may be formulated. And
thus radical theology may force theologians and biblical scholars
to appropriate in a really radical way the gospel of the kingdom
of God, without eliminating the element of its futurity and without circumventing its historical foundations in Jesus of Nazareth
and the witness to his resurrection. There is no question here of
repristinating an orthodox version of Christianity, whether we
think in terms of the patristic period or of the Protestant Reformation, for it must be remembered that orthodox Christianity
very quickly lost the eschatological dynamics of the gospel. The
full force of the eschatological dimension was diminished in favor
of static ontological thought forms and static ontocratic[13] institutions. And as much as I would like the contrary to be true, the
Reformation did not go the whole distance in penetrating to the
eschatological core and content of the biblical message.

II

FORSAKING GOD FOR THE SAKE OF MAN

Radical theology mistakenly believes that to pave the way for
a new birth of man, for a man who is liberated from the past and
open to the future, it is essential to proclaim the "death of God."
God must die to make room for man. God gets in the way of the
future of man. Rabbi Richard Rubenstein, the one and only Jewish "death of God" theologian in America, has observed that the
Protestant radicals are presently impaled on an either/or:
"Either God or man but not both."[14] The advent of a new hu-

[13] "Ontocratic" is used in the sense of Arend Th. van Leeuwen, *Christianity in World History,* tr. by H. H. Hoskins (Charles Scribner's Sons, 1964),
who uses it primarily to characterize the Eastern cultures which include all
reality—nature, man, and God—within a metaphysical unity of being. In
the Constantinian type of Christianity in the West, the Church and its institutions became part of the imperial order, a kind of cult which invoked the
absolute to cement the diverse elements of culture into a unity.
[14] Richard L. Rubenstein, *After Auschwitz: Essays in Contemporary
Judaism* (The Bobbs-Merrill Company, 1966), p. 248.

manity can only be inaugurated by ridding man of his chief hindrance to fulfillment. God-riddance is good news to man! But why? Why is it necessary to forsake God for the sake of the future and the freedom of man? Is this anything more than the vengeful antithesis of a Christianity which has so often been accused of forsaking man for the sake of God? What kind of a God is it who must be gotten rid of to make it possible for man to breathe the fresh air of hope for his future and fulfillment? Such a God would be a tyrant, an enemy of humanization. He would have to be a Moloch who requires man to immolate himself on the altars of what has been. Or he would have to be a lame-duck deity who possessed neither will nor skill to make a particle of difference for the better in human existence and world history. He would have to be a stationary God "up there" who had lost his freedom and his future. That is to a great extent the case with the inertial deity whom the radical theologians wish to entomb.

Gabriel Vahanian

The symbol of the "death of God" covers a wide range of interpretations. All of them begin with a view of man and the world in relation to which God must appear as an outside intruder, and therefore a misfit in the world of space and time, as a despotic ruler, and therefore an enemy of humanization, or simply as a non-essential hypothesis, and therefore as an inevitable casualty of Occam's razor in a scientific age. In 1961 Gabriel Vahanian published a book entitled *The Death of God: The Culture of Our Post-Christian Era*. He did not intend the main title to be taken literally, and so offered the subtitle as its interpretation. The "death of God" was a literary expression of a cultural event. Modern man is culturally incapacitated for the experience or knowledge of God. Vahanian's voice has been the wailing of a Kierkegaardian-Barthian in the wilderness of a culture which has lost the sense of transcendence. The immanentalism of modern culture, exhibited as much in its religiosity as in its secularism, locked God out of his world. Who is this God? He is the totally other, transcendent God of early dialectical theology. What kind of transcendence? A vertical transcendence which pictures God as hovering threateningly overhead. One can hear the unmistakable echoes of the Calvinistic *finitum non capax infiniti* reverberating through Vahanian's cultural diagnosis and his images of transcendence. One has to wonder, therefore, whether it is specifically *our* culture, and not any culture whatsoever, that would have difficulty bearing sacramental witness to a God whose utter transcendence abhors the limits of finitude. The sovereign absolute who stands outside the "culture of our post-Christian era" has all the telltale marks of being the "God up there." The modern man is correspondingly pictured as one who regrettably has lost interest in the numinous world above.

Vahanian does not say that God is really dead. He believes in the total transcendence of this totally-other God, in spite of the fact that our post-Christian culture makes that quite impossible and meaningless. But he does not tell us by what sort of trick he personally manages to do the impossible. What sort of ladder does he use to get from here below to the transcendent world above, even if that amounts to no more than the bare notion that there is somewhere an infinitely transcendent God whose absence from our culture is a matter for regret? Presumably he cannot leap out of our culture. Not even faith is able to do that. What is the content of Christian faith today if there is really no nail in our culture that keeps God and the world from falling completely apart in a dualistic manner? If God is essentially transcendent in the same sense in which our culture is totally incapable of any awareness of transcendence, then what sense does it make to speak of God? What meaning is there in being a Christian believer? It seems that one can only find refuge for faith in some sort of irrationalism, some new version of the *credo quia absurdum est.*

Why has Vahanian reached such an impasse? The answer, I believe, is to be found in his non-historical and non-eschatological symbolization of transcendence and immanence, of eternity and time, of God and the world. It is a Greek view of transcendence in a culture that is now radically de-Hellenized. It may be that tears are being shed in vain. The conclusion that "God is dead" culturally speaking may not have been reached at all had Vahanian seen that although our era has lost its passion for a world above this world, it does have a passion for the future. This might have suggested an opening toward a redefinition of transcendence, more in line with the idea of eschatological futurity of God in the Bible. The sense of the coming of the future in its creative power gives us an image of God as out in front of this world. For modern man transcendence will be understandable in terms of his orientation to the future or not at all. And the transcendence of God will have to be eschatologically reconceived within the horizon of historical possibilities that open upon a boundless future. The boundlessness of man's own future will be thought of as grounded in the future itself as a divine mode of being. To do this we will have to dispose of the idea that the future is but an imitation of the past and a repetition of the present. The future does not grow out of the past; the present cannot be projected into the future as its determinate content. The future entails exodus into something new; it may be conceived as the source of novelty and creativity. The newness of the new age is not just like making over an old suit of clothes. The challenge of the future ought to be grasped by theology as the occasion to carry through a revolution in its own conceptualizing of the transcendence of God in relation to modern man's sense of openness to the future of his world.

Paul van Buren

Two years after the appearance of Vahanian's book, Paul van Buren published *The Secular Meaning of the Gospel*. Like Vahanian he is of Barthian descent, but he takes quite the opposite turn. Instead of holding on to a God who lies absolutely beyond our culture, he lets go of God, holds on to our culture, and draws the conclusion that "God" has become for us a meaningless word. By his own admission van Buren is not a "death of God" theologian. That would involve him in the nonsensical assertion that God once lived. He states, "Today, we cannot even understand the Nietzschean cry that 'God is dead!' for if it were so, how could we know? No, the problem now is that the *word* 'God' is dead."[15] This statement makes it clear that van Buren's theology is the most unqualifiedly a-theistic of all the radical theologies we will discuss. He will have nothing to do with the mythical

[15] Paul van Buren, *The Secular Meaning of the Gospel*, p. 103.

idea that once upon a time in the distant past there was a living God, but sometime or other he died. The Christian who is also a secular man can make sense of the gospel, or the biblical story, only by deleting all talk of God. "The empiricist in us finds the heart of the difficulty not in what is said about God, but in the very talking about God at all."[16] Another citation: "We do not know 'what' God is, and we cannot understand how the word 'God' is being used."[17] To speak of God acting in the world is ruled out by the empirical criterion of meaning and truth which the secular man of our culture inevitably uses. Even to soften the blunt assertion that a supernatural God intervenes in any empirically real way in the world of human affairs, to say, for example, that we are speaking symbolically or analogically of God, is for van Buren merely to place a veil of pseudo-meaning over a meaningless statement. It won't work because it will "die the death of a thousand qualifications."[18]

The task of the Christian theologian is to use the method of linguistic analysis to translate "God-statements" into "many informative assertions about how things are with the world statements."[19] Religious language does not involve us in making outside, only about how things are with man on the inside.[20] Once the language of Christian faith has been stripped of its metaphysical and mythological elements, that is, all talk of being and God, only such statements will remain that share in the logic of the language of history and morals. The Christian is one who has an historical perspective centering in Jesus of Nazareth: this perspective shapes his moral commitments. To the query whether there is not more to it than that, van Buren responds, "In a secular age, what would that 'more' be?"[21] That

[16] *Ibid.*, p. 84.
[17] *Ibid.*
[18] It was Antony Flew who stated that "a fine brash hypothesis may thus be killed by inches, the death of a thousand qualifications": "Theology and Falsification," *New Essays in Philosophical Theology,* ed. by Antony Flew and Alasdair MacIntyre (The Macmillan Company, 1955), p. 97.
[19] Paul van Buren, *op. cit.,* p. 103.
[20] *Ibid.*, p. 171.
[21] *Ibid.*, p. 198.

is surely a fair question. Is there more to the Christian faith than a backward look to the historical Jesus and a high moral attitude inspired by him? Is the gospel more than a moral outlook with an historical reference to the man Jesus?

Paul van Buren asserts that there are three pieces to his theological puzzle:[22] (1) the conservative concern for the gospel of Christ, (2) the liberal concern for contemporary relevance, and (3) the logical analysis of theological statements. The third one is a methodological tool; it should not determine the sum and substance of theology. The second is most praiseworthy, and should be the concern of every vital theology. But what about the first, the conservative concern for the gospel of Christ? I do not know why the concern for christology, or a christological gospel, should be called "conservative." Was it not the tradition of liberal Protestant theology, running from Schleiermacher through Ritschl, which first elevated the rank of christology in theology? Were they not the first really christocentric theologians? In any case, it is not the claim to christocentricity as such, but rather the definition of the gospel which divides the spirits. What makes the gospel really gospel is not its christocentricity, for a law is equally capable of being centered in Christ. As Luther feared, Christ may easily be turned into a "second Moses" if we do not know what the gospel is. What does van Buren understand by the gospel? One has to look in vain for any grasp of the eschatological character of the New Testament gospel in van Buren's book. This is a more serious lack than the fact that the secular consciousness to which he is indebted is totally lacking the futurological dimension. Van Buren writes as though he had not learned that the gospel will not yield up its futuristic eschatology to a demythologizing exegesis, without losing what is essential in it. Nor will the secular consciousness of modern man be read in any depth without its creative drive toward the future. Hence, van Buren's logical analysis would have had different results had the language of hope and the future been kept in mind. His commitment to the later Wittgenstein might have urged him to explore the inherent logic of future-directed language,

[22] *Ibid.,* p. 18.

the language of hope which looks intently for the arrival of the creative future, without sacrificing religious language to the canons of scientific empiricism or moral perspectivism.

The "God" of the gospel has become a meaningless word to van Buren for several reasons. First, he has no longer any confidence in the ability of natural theology to give the word any meaning. The road of natural theology, he feels, has been marked by a dead-end sign by the work of Karl Barth.[23] Secondly, the self-definition of God in raising Jesus from the dead is muted by the denial that such an event really happened. If the resurrection of Jesus is the eschatological event of history by which God defines his meaning, then van Buren is at least being consistent in denying both at once. For the Christian, the belief that Jesus is still dead comes quite close to saying that "God" is meaningless. Had van Buren succeeded in giving a new definition of God, apart from his self-definition as the God of hope in the resurrection of Jesus, he would simply have started a new religion. The meaning of God and the gospel is bound up with Jesus and his resurrection. This interconnection was seen already by Jean Paul, the romantic poet, in his vision of the dead Christ who announces that there is no God. Moltmann has directed our attention to the profound significance of Jean Paul's vision for modern times, and especially for Christian theology. "The setting of Jean Paul's piece is the hour of the Last Judgment. The Christ who is awaited by the dead comes and proclaims: 'There is no God. I was mistaken. Everywhere is only stark, staring nothing, the death rigour of infinity. Eternity lies in chaos, gnaws at it and turns self-ruminant.' This vision is like a commentary on 1 Cor. 15:13ff. Hence it is significant that the message, 'There is no God,' is proclaimed in terms of despair of the hope of resurrection. It is plain that for Jean Paul the reality of God and the hope of resurrection depend on each other both for faith and unbelief."[24]

The meaning of the word "God" is bound to fade out when the essential medium of its meaning in the Christian faith is rendered speechless. The riches of the gospel become the rags of the law without the hope for new life pledged and promised by

---

[23] *Ibid.*, p. 98.
[24] J. Moltmann, *Theology of Hope*, p. 168.

God in the resurrection of Jesus. The "secular meaning" of the gospel gives to modern man what he already has enough of—law. The theological confusion of law and gospel is reinforced by a basic logical blunder. The eschatological language of the gospel is equated with the language of morals. He says, "Now the use of 'end-words' is to inform the hearer of, or to commend to him, a certain attitude of the speaker."[25] The attitude expressed by using eschatological language is verified by the conduct of the person who uses such language. Is this so? Immanuel Kant observed in his *Critique of Pure Reason* that there are three distinguishable orders of questions: 1. What can I know? 2. What ought I to do? 3. What may I hope?[26] The third is not the same question as the second. Has not van Buren made the logical mistake of reducing the language of hope to the language of moral intent and purpose? It just is not true to the interior logic of the language of either eschatology or ethics to collapse one into the other. "End-words" have been converted into "ought-words" and nothing more. It is true enough that we can get to the ethics of Jesus only by way of his eschatology, but the eschatology is not so much scaffolding that can be discarded once we reach the ethics.

William Hamilton

William Hamilton considers himself a hard-boiled radical who really means it when he says that "God is dead." His position, however, has been in continual flux from the beginning. To keep pace with the changing tempo of his mind, he has adopted the style of the "fragmentist."[27] It almost seems that to believe the same thing two years in a row is feared as a threatening sign of senility. Starting from the idea of the otherness and hiddenness of God, he went on to speak of the eclipse or the absence of God, then finally to the death of God as an historical event and an article of faith. Who is this God who has died? He is de-

[25] Paul van Buren, *op. cit.*, p. 131.
[26] Immanuel Kant, *Critique of Pure Reason* (London: J. M. Dent & Sons, 1934), p. 457.
[27] William Hamilton, "Thursday's Child," *op. cit.*, p. 89.

scribed, of course, in the terms in and through which Hamilton
once believed in him. These terms tell us which God has died. He
is the God of the past and the God of the gaps; he is the metaphysical "need-filler" and the religious "problem-solver." In the
place of this now dispensable God, Hamilton posits Jesus who
gives a man all the orientation he needs for this life. There is
no big need in man for which a God is needed. There is no
religious *a priori*. "There is no God-shaped blank within
man."[28] It is no longer necessarily true that man's heart is
restless until it finds its rest in God, as Augustine put it.
There are unmistakable echoes of the later Bonhoeffer to be
heard here, but Hamilton is not worried by the question
whether he is being true to the whole range of Bonhoeffer's
meaning. As he himself has admitted, "We are making a creative
misuse of Bonhoeffer."[29] With God gone, why stick with
Jesus? Hamilton never really answers that, except in such
confessional terms as, "I have a hang-up on Jesus." I think
he means that for himself personally, it is important to understand Jesus in order to understand better what his own life
is about. Is this merely an emotional fixation, or are there
reasonable grounds for it? If Jesus cannot be trusted to show
us the Father, if he lived under the spell of so fundamental
an illusion to his last breath on the cross, why should we trust
him for his ethic?

There are two sides to Hamilton's thinking that break in
half from the viewpoint of eschatology. While he was a "soft
radical" he could say, "We are not talking about the absence
of the experience of God, but of the experience of the absence
of God."[30] During this phase of mind he pictured the believer
as a waiting man, hoping for the return of God in a permanent
presence. In a moving passage he wrote, "We know too little
to know him now; we only know enough to be able to say that
he will come, in his own time, to the broken and contrite
heart, if we continue to offer that to him. Faith is, for many
of us, we might say, purely eschatological. It is a kind of trust

---

[28] W. Hamilton, "The Death of God Theologies Today," *ibid.*, p. 40.
[29] Based on a personal conversation with William Hamilton.
[30] W. Hamilton, "The Death of God Theologies Today," *op. cit.*, p. 28.

that one day he will no longer be absent from us. Faith is a cry to the absent God; faith is hope."[31] Hamilton lacked the patience of hope during this time of waiting "for what we do not see" (Rom. 8:25). At any rate, for some reason (Hamilton says it happened when he turned forty) a break occurred in his thinking. The element of expectancy, of hope, dropped clear out of sight. The conviction hardened that God is gone forever. "The death of God radicals are men without God . . . who do not anticipate his return."[32] This is the exact opposite of what he had said a few years before about hoping for the return and full presence of God. He entered upon a phase of hope-lessness, with no sense of an open future. This mood was soon exchanged for another, but here is what he said during this period: "Hope is the way of declaring one's future to be open and assured, and love is the way of standing before your neighbor in the present moment. Taking faith, hope, and love together, the feeling is that the American theologian can really live in only one of them at a time, perhaps only one in a lifetime. If this is so, and if it is also so that as an American he is fated to be a man without a sense of past or future, then it follows that the theologian today and tomorrow is a man without faith, without hope, with only the present, with only love to guide him."[33]

What do such words mean? They mean, I think, that the initial shock of experiencing the "death of God" led Hamilton to declare the end to any hope for the future. What Hamilton rightly saw at this moment was that to say that "God is dead," that hope has dried up, and that the future is closed, all amount to the same thing. The apostle Paul glimpsed this connection when he spoke of pagans as those "having no hope without God in the world."[34] Take away hope, remove the future, and the result is that "God is dead." Then man does not live in hopeful anticipation toward the future. He cannot be open

---

[31] W. Hamilton, *The New Essence of Christianity* (Association Press, 1961), p. 64.

[32] W. Hamilton, "American Theology, Radicalism, and the Death of God," *Radical Theology and the Death of God*, p. 6.

[33] W. Hamilton, "Thursday's Child," *op. cit.*, p. 87.

[34] Eph. 2:12.

beyond himself, to press beyond the limits of his own existence, to cross over frontiers, to long for and reach out toward
objects of hope to be realized in the future. Such a man becomes paralyzed, immobilized, in short, dead.

Hope-lessness, however, is a condition a man cannot for
long endure. Man will have his objects of hope or he will
invent them anew. Hamilton himself soon came to this realization, for within only two years of embracing his hope-less
and future-less vision for theology, he completely reversed
his position in "The New Optimism."[35] He declares now that
the dominant mood of modern culture is optimistic and hopeful about its possibilities. The future is open and malleable
to positive hopes. The hope that all things can be changed
for the better is becoming contagious again, symbolized first
by Kennedy's "New Frontier" and then by Johnson's "Great
Society." Pessimism is now out of date, culturally and theologically.
The old liberal doctrine of progress may even enjoy a comeback.
Tragedy has become a cultural impossibility.

All these blessings are ours, Hamilton thinks, because
"God is dead." But what about the still inevitable future of
our having to die? Buoyed up by this new optimism ·Hamil-
ton assures us that we can face "death not with the hope for
immortality, but with the human confidence that man may
befriend death and live with it as a possibility alongside."[36]
The future for man which Hamilton now envisions is not
grounded in the power of God's future to make all things
new but in the possibilities that exist already in the present. This is a present, however, from which all negativities
have been removed by wishful thinking. The future is viewed
now as a mere extension of the present, and thus lacks the creativity of the future of God that broke open the way of hope
through the resurrection of Jesus from the dead. In the span
of a few years we have seen Hamilton's theology flip-flopping
from hope without faith, to love without hope, and at last to
hope without faith. This is so, perhaps, because a person's
subjective moods are in fact that variable and shifting. If

[35] In *Radical Theology and the Death of God,* pp. 157ff.
[36] *Ibid.,* p. 169.

subjectivity is the source of theology, Hamilton is doing as well as can be expected.

Richard Rubenstein

The condition of man, as Hamilton now views it, is such that even if God were real, he would be irrelevant. In Rabbi Richard Rubenstein we find exactly the opposite feeling. If God really existed, there would be plenty for him to do. The trouble is, he is not doing anything. The tragic sense of life, the absurdity of suffering, the horror chambers and death camps of the twentieth century are proof that we live in a time of the "death of God." The God of history must be dead, or else he would have to be the ultimate author of the death of six million Jews. "After Auschwitz" Jews can no longer believe in a *Heilsgeschichte* in which they, as the chosen people, play a central role in the drama of a God who acts redemptively in history. "After the experience of our times, we can neither affirm the myth of the omnipotent God of history nor can we maintain its corollary, the election of Israel. After the death camps, the doctrine of Israel's election is in any event a thoroughly distasteful pill to swallow."[37]

The Nazi death camps make it impossible for Rubenstein to enjoy the new-found optimism of Hamilton. The motifs of existentialism—anxiety and nothingness, absurdity and tragedy—picture man as a lonely drifter toward death in a cold, unfeeling, and indifferent cosmos. There is no plot in history, no role for me. Death is the Messiah. The only God is Holy Nothingness from whence we come and whither we go. Meanwhile? We have religion. And herein lies the irony of Rubenstein's position. Whereas the Protestant radicals, echoing the later Bonhoeffer, call for a religionless Christianity as a direct consequence of the demise of deity, Rubenstein sees so much the greater need for religion at such a time. What else do we have to comfort us in the crises of life? Rubenstein claims that the real problem is not how to speak of God without religion, but how to speak of religion without God. "In the time of the death of God,

[37] Richard Rubenstein, *After Auschwitz*, p. 69.

I suspect we need rituals to dramatize and celebrate the crises of life more than ever."[38]

"Since the God of history is dead, we will have to return to a religion of nature. We will come to know once again the primitive earth-deities, Baal and Astarte, whom Israel forsook to become Jahweh's chosen people with a mission in history."[39] (Rubenstein seems to have ignored the fact that it was precisely the turn to earth-deities of "Blut und Boden" in Nazi Germany which paved the way for Hitler to send six million Jews to the death camps. It is the resurgence of the religion of nature, and not loyalty to the God of history, which nourishes the racial myths of the twentieth century, first directed against the Jews and now against Negroes.) In any case, Rubenstein does not see the return of the house of Jacob to the land of Israel in our century as one of the latest in the series of the mighty acts of God. It is just a decision of a people to "return to earth" after a wretched experience of wandering in the wilderness of history, driven madly by the illusion of having a unique mission and destiny. This illusion, this historical myth, has been the source of so much of Israel's misery. It also helps to explain the peculiar hatred which Christians, who claim to be the new Israel, have shown toward Jews.

Rubenstein's position instructs us, once again, of the close correlation between the "death of God" as a theological phenomenon and the loss of the eschatological horizon of historical experience. The rabbi's refrain is that man is really without hope, with only death to greet him in the future toward which he is groping in fear. This existential anticipation of death as the eschaton recoils upon life in the present, creating spasms of anxiety and cramps of futility. With an expression of pain, quite unlike the other "death of God" men, Rubenstein confesses, "I cannot rejoice in the death of God. If I am a death-of-God theologian, it is with a cry of agony."[40] The purpose of religion is to fill the void created

[38] *Ibid.*, p. 235.
[39] *Ibid.*, pp. 70, 136.
[40] *Ibid.*, p. 263.

by God's disappearance, to give some relief for unbelief. Rabbi Rubenstein is calling for a clear choice between the gods of nature and the God of history. The gods of nature are symbols of comfort. The God of history is the author of an exodus community with a mission to the nations. The missionary existence of God's people, spurred on by a militant eschatological consciousness, creates abrasive encounters and even catastrophic turning points in history. The price of peace with the world is the abandonment of this mission, the return to the "flesh pots of Egypt." The temptation is there. The New Testament story of Christ struggles with exactly the sorts of issues of suffering and tragedy with which Rabbi Rubenstein so earnestly deals. Both God and man are in need of justification to each other in this kind of world. The mission of Israel and her election cannot be understood and endured without the cross of the Messiah and the promise for new life that is given in the resurrection of Jesus.

III
TOWARD AN ESCHATOLOGICAL HUMANISM

Our discussion of radical theology to this point has explored possible connections between the "death of God" phenomenon and the loss of the eschatological horizon in modern theology. Might it not be that eschatology is the key to the recovery of a doctrine of God "after the death of God"? The phrase "after the death of God" means that the new conditions of our era which precipitated the present crisis in theological understanding cannot willfully be ignored in the interest of repristinating some traditional doctrines. It may be that some doors have been shut by radical theology; it may also be that a new opening is being hinted at from the side of our secular world, first by the futuristic tendencies in our culture, and secondly by the emergence of a philosophy of hope (Chapter 3). Every creative theology has involved a vital response to the challenge of its situation. The futurological trends in modern thought may become the occasion to activate the eschatological origins of the Christian faith in our time. The focal point of a correlation between a theology of the future and secular futurism is the quest for the truly human and the good society. Can a true humanism be established on any other grounds than the eschatological disclosure of the shape of a new humanity in the person of Jesus? The future of Christian theology will be decided, to a great extent, by whether it can put its eschatology to work in favor of the secular quest for true humanization.

Thomas Altizer

Thomas Altizer is the most thoroughgoing eschatological thinker among the radical theologians. The aim of his theology is "to apprehend the Christian meaning of the kingdom of God in a situation in which God is dead."[41] That is a paradoxical assertion. For Altizer, however, the "death of God" is itself an eschatological event, a saving event, the good news of the gospel itself. It is cause for rejoicing. Why? Because it makes possible the forward-moving process of history. If God stands outside the process as a fixed transcendent reality, he slows down the process. If he joins the process by a total self-negation, by a kenotic metamorphosis, the effect is to speed up the process. God gets rid of himself for the sake of man. Altizer can acknowledge that "the biblical God is the God of the End"[42] who puts an end to himself. He annihilates himself, first in the flesh of Jesus, and then in the immanental Word of the historical process itself. No wonder that Altizer is moved to criticize the doctrine of God in modern theology as its weakest link.[43] He is thinking especially of Barth and Tillich. In attaching themselves to traditional images and expressions from the past, their minds lagged behind the eschatological event of God's death. Indeed, it often seems that the God whose death Altizer calls upon us to affirm is none other than Barth's "Wholly Other" and Tillich's "Ground of Being."

[41] Thomas Altizer, "Nirvana and the Kingdom of God," *New Theology No. 1* (The Macmillan Company, 1964), p. 155.

[42] *Ibid.*, p. 154.

[43] *Ibid.*, p. 151.

Altizer's harsh judgment on any Christian theology that remains anchored in the past is due to his own special blending of the apocalyptic eschatology of the Bible and Hegel's principle of negativity. For Altizer authentic eschatological thinking requires not merely freedom from the heteronomous authority of the past and the regressions of faith it evokes, but even a radical negation of the historic expressions of the Word of God in Jesus of Nazareth and the primitive Christian community. He believes that biblical eschatology and Hegel's negativity principle call for a total alienation of the present from the past, a complete rupture by which the past is denied participation in the eschatological reality of the future.[44]

The most serious result of Altizer's negation of the past is the fate of Jesus in his system. Jesus is not for him the eschatological event without equal. As a past event of history he is one of the stations that gets left behind as the eschatological train of reality moves ahead. The eschatological future of mankind has not already been previewed in Jesus, as the gospel of his resurrection declares. The plain reason for this is that Altizer denies the resurrection. It is a religious myth that comes from paganism, and leads Christianity back into paganism wherever it is believed. There is some consistency at this point in Altizer's thought, for to have affirmed the resurrection of Jesus without seeing it as the promise of God for the future of man would have put asunder what the earliest Christian tradition has joined together. He would have had to accord a role of permanent significance to the Jesus of history. Altizer makes up for the loss of the Jesus of history by the contemporariness of Christ as the Word. This Christ can be contemporary without the resurrection of Jesus from the dead because he has nothing whatsoever to do with the Jesus of history.

Altizer was a student of Paul Tillich. Tillich always spoke of "Jesus as the Christ." The little word "as" held the name and the title together in an always fragile dialectic. In Altizer the two terms fall apart. The drive toward gnosticism which Tillich always re-

[44] T. Altizer, "Word and History," *Radical Theology and the Death of God*, p. 133.

sisted in his thinking gains uninhibited expression in Altizer. Altizer acknowledged that "Tillich is the modern father of radical theology,"[45] but he attacked him at every decisive point. In his criticism of Tillich's christology he states: "The Christ who is an 'answer' to our condition must be a wholly immanent Word that is fully detached from the Jesus of history."[46] Tillich's "God" must be removed for the sake of the future of man, and the factual basis of the biblical picture of the Christ must be obliterated from memory for the sake of the present.

The concern of Christian faith for the Jesus of history is grounded in his final significance for the future of mankind. If he is not the incarnation of the eschatological fulfillment of mankind, there is no reason why theology should remain attached to Jesus of Nazareth—except by force of habit. Altizer wants us to break that habit. But then why should the new religion of the present that cuts itself off from all past expressions continue to think of itself as in any sense a legitimate continuation of the historic Christian faith? What makes the new religion of the present Christian? It cannot be the principle of mere contemporaneity. The communist party is as contemporary and so is the Ku Klux Klan. There are plenty of brand new religions just as contemporary as Altizer's vision of a new Christianity. There would have to be also a principle of continuity. But Altizer seems to have destroyed that possibility by his total rejection of the past. If the past has become void of meaning for our present, then our present itself is emptied of meaning as soon as the future arrives to condemn it to the past. Altizer's eschatology, in the last analysis, is a gnostic flight out of history. Altizer has not seen that the past and the present may be oriented upon the same horizon of the future, and derive their positive meaning for each other by their relation to it. And what is this future? For Christian faith, which Altizer also claims to affirm, it is the future of Jesus the Messiah, who has already been made known to us through the traditions of the gospel. Without the

[45] T. Altizer, *The Gospel of Christian Atheism*, p. 10
[46] T. Altizer, "America and the Future of Theology," *op. cit.*, p. 11.

representative role of Jesus in pioneering our future through his cross and resurrection, the future becomes a terrifying reality with nothing but the power to negate all that has gone before. Then death or nothing-ness becomes the lord of the universe. Because Altizer's eschatology functions only as a principle of negation, the linkage of meaning between past and present and future, which for Christian faith has been forged by the advent of the eschatological future in the Messiah Jesus, has been shattered beyond repair.

The result of Altizer's negativistic eschatology is anti-humanistic. Without attachment to the new manhood of the Messiah Jesus, he loses the ability to discern the traces of new life in history. The eschatological future cannot create positive prolepses in history of the final fulfillment in the kingdom of God. Hence, Altizer's eschatology lacks any specifiable normative content in history. He is bound to affirm whatever the future brings into the present. Recently that future has brought such monstrous evils as Hiroshima, Dachau, and Vietnam. Altizer's futurism destroys the foundations of a true humanism because it has alienated itself from the proleptic inauguration of the ultimate future of mankind in the Messiah Jesus, *vere homo,* the new man of the future. Altizer admits that he has nothing to say about the horrendous social and political crises of the twentieth century. His eschatological visions give birth to no ethical impulses or imperatives. His apocalyptic dreams become fuzzy because he chooses to do his gazing into an empty future, not the future that frames the picture of Jesus and the kingdom of his Father, not the future refracted through the prismatic of Jesus' cross and resurrection. This accounts also for the fact that Altizer sees little to choose between the Nirvana of Buddhism and the kingdom of God in the message of Christianity.[47]

Harvey Cox

If Altizer's eschatology has lost all footing in the history of promise, its focus on the Jesus of history, and its concern

[47] T. Altizer, "Nirvana and the Kingdom of God," *op. cit.*

for the future of man, Harvey Cox is trying to rediscover the eschatological initiatives for a true humanism and the shape of a new society. We could say that by moving toward the philosophy of Ernst Bloch and the theology of Jürgen Molt-mann, he is pointing the way toward an eschatological human-ism beyond the "death of God." If eschatology and humanism have fallen apart in Altizer, Cox is trying to reunite them in a doctrine of God in which the category of future is primary.

The two shakiest features in Cox's famous book, *The Secu-lar City,* were his doctrine of God and his eschatology. His plea that we disengage our language about God from the meta-physical theism encasing the Christian tradition was not matched in clarity by an alternative proposal. Cox too eas-ily assumed that we could move directly from Yahweh of the Bible to "speak in a secular fashion of God."[48] He as-serted that traditional categories are bankrupt. But he did not show why it is that biblical categories should be any less bankrupt for modern man. At this time he was groping toward a new doctrine of God which would be congruent with an under-standing of the world as history. The eschatology of history that was operative in his book did not as yet provide him with the key to such a doctrine. Eschatology was too quickly identi-fied with the process of secularization. Many feared that for Cox the New Jerusalem is nothing more than the secular city. Our experience of the secular city, while exhilarating, has not been all that fulfilling.

Since the publication of *The Secular City,* Harvey Cox has begun to explore the closer connections between escha-tology and a theology after the "death of God" phase which is now coming to an end. He dissociates himself from the Christian atheists, but he is grateful that by closing certain doors, they have pushed him to the future. "They have turned

---

[48] See Cox's later admission: "I still believe that the problem of speaking in a secular fashion of God has important sociological and political aspects. But I believe it has theological dimensions far more baffling than those indicated in *The Secular City*": "Afterword," *The Secular City Debate,* ed. by Daniel Callahan (The Macmillan Company, 1966), p. 203.

my face toward the future, where if man meets God again, that encounter must take place."[49] They have thoroughly exposed the crisis in the doctrine of God. Theirs is a call for new directions. The way ahead is to take up the theme of the future in theology as a governing principle. On a prophetic note he has stated, "The only future that theology has . . . is to become the theology of the future." New light along this way shines from the thought of two philosophers, Teilhard de Chardin and Ernst Bloch. "The way out of the 'death of God' miasma which leads forward rather than backward is lighted . . . by two of the seminal minds of our era, Pierre Teilhard de Chardin and Ernst Bloch."[50] Cox is now saying that the question of God must be focused on the issues of man's future. Teilhard's ideas about the humanization of man and the hominization of the universe, and Bloch's idea of religion as hope and his ontology of not-yet being, stir up memories of a forgotten heritage in the Christian past. A new symbol of the transcendence of God may be imagined by reconceiving it "in terms of the pressure exerted by the future on the present."[51] Both Teilhard and Bloch "see the future as that pressure on the present which is only possible where there is a creature who can orient himself toward the future and relate himself to reality by this orientation, in short a 'creature who can hope'."[52]

By turning to the future in theology Harvey Cox has taken the initiative in presenting a new option, more in harmony with the American feeling for reality as a project to be worked at with promise for the future. He is pointing a way beyond "the theological dead end signaled by the death-of-God theologians."[53] It is a sign of health if theology is once again looking to the future, to meet the God who is coming, the God of promise and hope, of exodus and resurrection, even though this creates the difficult assignment of refashioning

[49] *Ibid.*
[50] Harvey Cox, "The Death of God and the Future of Theology," *On Not Leaving It to the Snake* (London: SCM Press, 1968), p. 8.
[51] *Ibid.*
[52] *Ibid.*, pp. 8-9.
[53] Harvey Cox, "Afterword," *The Secular City Debate*, p. 202.

on this basis all our major theological categories. The present trend in Cox's thought points to a convergence with a similar direction in continental theology, which takes up the problem of the future as a new point of departure. The next two chapters will offer an examination of the philosophical and theological sides of this movement.

3

Ernst Bloch's Philosophy of Hope

Carl E. Braaten

The study of Ernst Bloch's philosophy became an important preliminary task on the way to writing my book, *The Future of God*. As atheistic humanism it is a challenge to Christian theology to undergird and articulate a fuller and more authentic humanism. The sub-title of Bloch's latest book, *Atheismus im Christentum,* goes like this: "Only an atheist can be a good Christian, only a Christian can be a good atheist." The sense in which this is true may come out in this chapter. Originally, it was given as an address at The American Academy of Religion, meeting in Chicago, February 20-21, 1970.

I

Toward a Philosophy of the Future

Ernst Bloch's philosophy of utopian hope is reaching its pinnacle of influence at a time when Western philosophy is in dire need of a "new metaphysic" and when theology needs to have its courage restored to take up its main theme of God and his kingdom in relation to the history of man and his world. Bloch wrote his first major work, *Geist der Utopie,* in 1918, the same year that Karl Barth began stirring up his new recipe for a theology of disengagement from philosphy. Most theologians did not respond to Barth's appeal. Bultmann led the way in establishing an intimate connection with Heidegger's philosophy of existence. Brunner latched on to Buber's I-Thou scheme of personal encounter. Tillich correlated philosophy and theology in terms of a question-and-answer dialectic; the *tertium*

59

comparationis was ultimately Schelling's philosophy of identity. A few theologians allied themselves with Whitehead's philosophy of organic process; the result so far has not been a clear interpretation of the Christian faith. Currently, Wittgenstein's philosophy of language is being explored by theologians as a help in understanding the logic of their own language tradition. The assumption of this procedure is positivistic; the language is there, it exists, there is nothing wrong with it, we only need to understand what it means as ordinary folks use it. The axe of Karl Marx is aimed at the roots of this assumption: "The philosophers have only interpreted the world . . . the point, however, is to *change* it."[1]

Bloch's philosophy of hope has not been a part of the running dialogue with theology during the last decades. It is only in recent years, since leaving East Germany in 1961, that a few theologians have begun to take notice of Bloch's philosophy of the future. The point of his philosophy is to change the world in the power of that ennobling future which attracts it beyond all that keeps it small and trivial in the present. Bloch's is a philosophy of change guided by the functions and objects of hope that are laid up in the future of reality on its way forward. He has constructed a "new metaphysic" which intends to give the primacy and priority to the future mode of being. In his words, this is an "ontology of being-that-is-not-yet."[2] The structure of his philosophy is determined by a fundamental correlation between a phenomenology of hope and an ontology of the future. No wonder that Christian theology should feel an affinity with this philosophy, in spite of its atheism, and find in it a challenge to rediscover its own foundations of hope in the movement of history from slavery to freedom, from the wilderness to the promised land, from death to life, from the old world to the new creation, from the realm of evil to the kingdom of God. This is a movement in history in which Bloch's fundamental categories of newness (*Novum*), the front-line (*Front*), and the future (*Zukunft*) find an atmosphere congenial to them.

---

[1] Quoted by Bernard Delfgaauw, *The Young Marx* (Newman Press, 1967), p. 50.

[2] Ontologie des Noch-Nicht Seins."

What is it, after all, that theology ought to seek from philosophy? What kind of contact is most justified and useful? It is to be hoped that Barth's injunction against theology's dependence on philosophy will not have been entirely in vain. For there is a kind of obsequious servility and expectant posturing before philosophy that only brings disgrace upon theology, and vice versa. On the other hand, a policy of co-existence in which neither does anything for the other is not tenable in the long run. For each has within itself a drive toward universality, and neither can respect boundaries that rest on arbitrary assertions. Here we are primarily concerned not with what theology can do for philosophy, but with what philosophy may do for theology.

Philosophy should drive theology more deeply into its own theme. It acts as a midwife when it serves well. This means that philosophy should not fix the mold in advance; it should not simply ask the question to which theology is to give the answers. It may not offer a closed system of categories in which theology must seek its own accommodation. One cannot help but think of the theological use of Heidegger.[3]

Philosophy is not a more rational translation of the primitive symbolic expressions of religion. It is not a higher gnosis, which patronizingly makes room for the religion of the *hoi polloi*. Philosophy has no authority over theology; it cannot dictate in an authoritarian manner from loftier heights of wisdom. Kierkegaard feared that Hegel's philosophy laid claim to such superiority. Philosophy should not switch theology onto another track, to lure it away from its own theme. It should not force theology to sell its birthright to appeal to the pace-setters of culture and cater to their ideas of the true, good and beautiful. Neo-Platonism has given theology a vertical shape at the expense of its own horizontal thrust forward toward the future. And Kantianism converted Christianity into a transcendental ethic.

Likewise, there is no perennial philosophy to which theol-

---

[3] See *Heidegger und die Theologie,* ed. by Gerhard Noller (München: Chr. Kaiser Verlag, 1967).

ogy has to revert, for the idea of perennialism itself belongs to a philosophy governed by the recurrencies of nature, rather than the contingencies of history. Nor can philosophy build a first story of natural knowledge, to which theology adds a second of supernatural mysteries. This is a ruling image of theology betraying the mark of its origin in a culture controlled by the ecclesiastic hierarchy. When neo-Thomism perpetuates the use of Aristotle's philosophy as natural theology in an age in which the cultural position of the hierarchy has collapsed, it greatly underestimates the historicity of thought itself, that is, the conditions of meaning and truth which are themselves historical, and therefore relative to the context in which they emerge.

Theology has made the right decision in seeking contacts, points of convergence and divergence, with all of these various philosophical systems. The test that must be applied in retrospect is whether a given philosophy has stimulated theology to express its own theme under the new conditions of experience and knowledge. The test is not whether theology echoes what philosophy knows on its own, but whether philosophy's vision of reality stirs the imagination of theology to go deeply into its own source and to find its own shape under the new conditions of experience and knowledge. Philosophers can keep theologians honest, not by demanding their submission to heteronomous criteria, but by encouraging them to be *theo*-logians, if that is what they claim to be. Theology, in turn, has a critical function, and that is to sight the internal contradictions of any philosophy, and to establish the truth and validity of its own claims at the point of these contradictions. There is an apologetic, even a polemical, function of theology which is given along with the universality implied by the eschatological factum on which theology is based. These formal aspects of the connection between theology and philosophy must be kept in mind when theology today enters into dialogue with the philosophy of Ernst Bloch. The first question is, then, whether this philosophy can arouse theology out of its slumbers, in neo-orthodoxy or existentialism, to take up its own theme of eschatology as the genesis of theology; and the second is whether theology has the capacity to disclose the inherent contradiction of this philosophy, and point the way to the clarifying truth and the fulfilling reality.

Ernst Bloch is the first philosopher who has elevated hope, and its correlate the future, to a place of prominence in philosophy. Heidegger, of course, also made the mode of future the primary category in his *Being and Time,* and challenged the static "ontology of extant being" *(Ontologie des Vorhandenen)* which underlies the history of Western philosophy. Heidegger overcame the "ontology of extant being" by defining existence in terms of openness to the future. But the future to which Heidegger refers is not the future of the world, but of human existence alone, and it is not a future of fulfillment but of death, not a basis of hope but a source of anxiety. In Heidegger the ultimate reality from which man and his world stand out *(ekstasis)* is nothing-ness. For Bloch there is hope for a transcending future fulfillment beyond the negativities and alienations in man and his society. Bloch attempts to give ontological footing to hope and the tendency of reality to open toward fulfillment in the future.

The future of philosophy, as Bloch sees it, is to become the philosophy of the future. Over a century ago the glimmerings of this idea appeared in the title of Ludwig Feuerbach's writing, *Principles of the Philosophy of the Future* (1843).[4] A similar hint is later contained in the sub-title of Nietzsche's *Beyond Good and Evil,* which reads "A Prelude to a Philosophy of the Future." Bloch states, "Philosophy will have a conscience for tomorrow, a bias for the future, a knowledge of hope, or it will no longer have any knowledge at all. And the new philosophy, as it was opened up by Marx, is the same thing as the philosophy of the new reality, which awaits us all, nullifying or fulfilling us."[5] Philosophy's concern is not mainly with what has been, but with what is to be—the *future* of reality. Philosophy must be concerned about the future of man, if philosophy is to integrate the question of praxis into its own theory.

[4] Ludwig Feuerbach, *Principles of the Philosophy of the Future,* tr. and with an Introduction by Manfred H. Vogel (The Bobbs-Merrill Company, 1966).

[5] Ernst Bloch, *Das Prinzip Hoffnung,* Vol. I, p. 5.

The task of philosophy is to teach hope as a way of thinking. Thought may be a reflection on things as they are, or, if it is driven by hope, it may cross beyond their boundaries through an anticipating consciousness. Thinking may transgress the present by anticipating the future. It may shake the present until it yields up something new, by jogging the tendencies that run deep in the nature of reality. Every man who strives lives from the future in hope. This elementary fact has been far too long ignored by philosophy. Philosophy has not worked up an appropriate system of concepts to express hope for the future. Philosophy has been dominated by the introspective or retrospective moods, leaving the prospective approach out of account. Man and his world are bound to the past, or go round and round in a cycle of recurrency. Knowledge since Plato has been recollective (*anamnesis*) or analytical; its proleptic or anticipatory dimension has not found its place in epistemology. "Longing, expectation, and hope need their own hermeneutic; the dawning of what is before us demands its specific concept, the new (*Novum*) requires its con-

  Docta spes, learned hope, is Bloch's theme. "Expectation, hope, cept of the frontier (*Frontbegriff*)."[6]

and intention in relation to possibility that is still unrealized: all this is not only a basic feature of the human consciousness, but, rightly understood, a basic definition of objective reality as a whole."[7] The subject-object correlation may be characterized by the relation between *spes qua speratur* and *spes quae speratur*.[8] Hope is not merely a subjective mood of man; it is a medium which discloses the dialectic of reality in its expedition in *terram utopicam*.[9] One might say, the mood is the medium and the message—a message about the movement of matter toward what it has not yet become (*Noch-Nicht-Gewordene*). So the fundamental theme of philosophy as a *Theorie-Praxis* is the transition through revolutionary conflict from the old to the new, from exile to homeland, from dreams of a better life in the future to their concrete realization. What Bloch presents to us is an inven-

[6] *Ibid.*
[7] *Ibid.*
[8] *Ibid.*, Vol. III, p. 1624.
[9] *Ibid.*, Vol. I, p. 6.

tory of man's hopes, an "encyclopedia of hopes."[10] And since "wherever there is hope, there is religion,"[11] Bloch draws heavily from the religious tradition, especially Jewish messianism, the historical prophecies of the Old and New Testaments, and the apocalyptic line in sectarian Christianity, as well as the modern secularized forms of the eschatological hopes in the Bible. "The eschatological consciousness came into the world from the Bible."[12] This is not to say that Bloch makes his philosophy dependent in any way on the Bible; rather, he finds there the images of hope which illustrate the "forwardism"[13] so deeply grooved in man and his world.

II
THE CATEGORIES OF "THE PRINCIPLE OF HOPE"

The core of Bloch's philosophy is the ontological status of the category of possibility. His ontology of the future is based on an analysis of this category, which he feels has never been given its due in the traditional table of categories. This category has an objective and a subjective side. Hope and anticipation are the ferment of the subjective pole of possibility. They are expressed at a superficial level, for example, in day-dreams. In day-dreams, in difference from night-dreams, the mind is filled with the pulse-beats of the future. They are not a regression to the past, a longing for a fabulous once-upon-a-time. These dreams expect the dawning of the future; they focus on possibilities in objective reality. Possibility discloses the world as changeable, in a state of flux, and open to the future. "It is only the horizon of the future . . . which gives to reality its real dimension."[14]

Bloch takes issue sharply with the underlying assumption in the Freudian interpretation of dreams. It is dominated by an

---

[10] *Ibid.*, p. 16.

[11] *Ibid.*, Vol III, pp. 1404, 1417.

[12] *Ibid.*, Vol. I, p. 254.

[13] Paul Tillich's term, "The Effects of Space Exploration on Man's Condition and Stature," *The Future of Religions*, p. 46. One of Bloch's favorite terms is "vorwärts."

[14] E. Bloch, *Das Prinzip Hoffnung*, Vol. I, p. 332.

ontology of recurrence to the past. Psychoanalysis sees the present as laden with memories of the past, or with a past which is pushed down into the cellar of the subconscious. It sees the struggle of the mind in terms of its relation to the past or the present, not in terms of an anticipatory leap forward to reality that still slumbers in the state of possibility. The real antithesis to hope is not fear, but memory. Psychoanalysis knows of the subconscious, the contents of which are tied to the past, but not of the foreconsciousness of the new which breaks forth from as yet unrealized possibilities.[15] The phenomenon of hunger, in the broadest sense, is a clue that man is not satisfied in the present by receiving merely a new interpretation of his past; he can be satisfied only by something new from the future, by something that has never yet happened to him and his world.

We have said that the elements of anticipation are part of reality itself; the will-to-utopia is correlative with the thrust forward in the objective world. Reality is process[16] in which the future becomes mediated through human decision, through social and political actions, in the present. Hope undergirds responsible action, a "militant optimism."[17] The positivistic attitude of empiricism is to be rejected because it begins and ends with an objectifying analysis of things as they are; it is blind to the future. The shallow empiricist is a fetishist of so-called facts; he does not see that their future determines their reality and meaning. In Bloch's dialectical logic, a thing is not what it is, but what it will be.[18] The essence of a thing is not in a world behind this world, or above it, in a Platonic heaven of ideas, but lies in its future. The reality of matter resides in its futurity; to be human is to have a utopia, to be in hope, ahead of oneself, to be in quest of one's essence and to establish it in the future. The future is the true place of fulfillment.

Militant optimism is on the front-line of the world process. The *Front* is the furthest edge of factual reality, the borderline

[15] *Ibid.*, pp. 61ff.
[16] *Ibid.*, pp. 225-226.
[17] *Ibid.*, p. 227.
[18] See on E. Bloch's logic, Adolph Lowe, "S ist noch nicht P," *Ernst Bloch zu ehren*, ed. by Siegfried Unseld (Frankfurt: Suhrkamp Verlag, 1965).

between reality and possibility. To bring about change in reality, one has to exert the necessary leverage at the *Front* where the future is being decided. The category of the *Front* is linked closely with the concept of newness, the *Novum*. The idea of newness "pervades the whole Bible, from Jacob's blessing to the Son of Man, who makes all things new, to the new heaven and the new earth."[19] Bloch interprets the Bible in his own peculiar way, but he certainly is not wrong in seeing that newness is the heart of its promise. As the history of promise moves from the Old Testament to the New, we hear more and more of a new covenant, a new Israel, a new Jerusalem, a new man, a new creation, a new life, a new heaven and a new earth—all sign-posts of the future and final coming of God's kingdom. Bloch ontologizes the idea of newness in the history of salvation.

Salvation is not an interior process that takes place within the heart of the individual; it is a world-historical process in which *all* things are being made new. Bloch likes to quote Rev. 21:5: "Behold, I make *all* things new." The "all" includes the world of matter and nature. The world is on its way to a *Novum,* which Bloch further characterizes by terms like *Ultimum, Totum, Universum,* and *Alles.* Not only man, but also history, not only history, but also nature—all are in motion to a kingdom of fullness and freedom, wholeness and unity. Salvation is not a backward movement, a *restitutio in integrum,* a return to pristine origins. It is a forward movement of the whole of reality—exodus into the promised land. Bloch describes the world as "a laboratory of possible salvation."[20] He can also speak of the reconciliation of man and nature—betraying no doubt the influence of Schelling's romantic philosophy of nature on his thought—as the "naturalization of man" and the "humanization of nature."[21] Bloch, however, redefines the concept of nature within the framework of dialectical materialism. In so doing he has altered the rigid concept of matter which became dominant in some Marxist circles, one which hearkened back to a mechanistic view of matter, a vulgar

[19] E. Bloch, *Das Prinzip Hoffnung,* Vol. I, p. 235.
[20] See the essay on Bloch by Fritz Vilmar, "Welt als Laboratorium Salutis," *Ernst Bloch zu ehren,* pp. 121-134.
[21] E. Bloch, *Das Prinzip Hoffnung,* Vol. I, p. 235.

materialism, as Bloch called it. Bloch was attacked by his fellow Marxists in East Germany and forced into premature retirement from his professorship primarily because he had a sense for the inner transcendence of matter and because of his concerns for personality and individuality, and for the humanizing dimensions of religion.

Nevertheless, Bloch is a materialist. Yet the question whether the materialist foundation of his thought places him in irreconcilable opposition to Christianity is not decided by the label itself. Archbishop William Temple's assertion that "Christianity is the most materialistic of all religions" has yet to be taken seriously as something more than a harmless aphorism. The assumption is still widespread that Christianity's innermost bias leans to spiritualism, that detachment from the world of matter and a vertical ascent of the soul are the same as the summons to enter the kingdom of God. It is not Bloch's materialism as such that sets him in conflict with Christianity, but the fact that his atheism forces him to entrust to matter what only God can be and do.

Matter is derived etymologically from *mater*, the Latin for "mother." Matter is thought of as the pregnant womb of mother-earth, yielding up her fruit in ever new and blessed forms, the highest of which is man himself. Bloch's decisive work on his concept of matter has not yet been published.[22] It appears, however, that his own concept of the future is finally shipwrecked by his materialism. The agency and direction of the dialectical world-process have to be built into matter from the beginning. The process of transcending goes on within matter, but there is no transcendence.[23] This jeopardizes Bloch's insistence on the ontological priority of the future: "The real genesis is not at the beginning, but at the end."[24] It is more than doubtful that a

---

[22] Entitled *Geschichte und Gehalt des Begriffs Materie*. Reference is made to this unpublished manuscript by Wolf-Dieter Marsch, in *Hoffen Worauf? Auseinandersetzung mit Ernst Bloch* (Hamburg: Furche-Verlag, 1963), p. 52.

[23] E. Bloch speaks of a "transzendierende ohne Transzendenz" in *Das Prinzip Hoffnung*, Vol. I, p. 166. Elsewhere he writes: "Es ist ein Transzendere ganz ohne Transzendenz." Quoted by Fritz Vilmar, "Welt als Laboratorium Salutis," *op. cit.*, p. 132.

[24] E. Bloch, *Das Prinzip Hoffnung*, Vol. III, p. 1628.

real eschatology of reality is possible within the framework of even so elastic and dynamized a concept of matter as Bloch has.

Bloch stands in an ambivalent relation to religion. Hope is the quintessence of religion insofar as religion is truly human. Religious symbols and stories express the profoundest hope of mankind for the ultimate fulfillment of history. At least, this is true of the Jewish and Christian religions. Messianism lies at their very core. The dehumanizing examples of religion are those which cause men to hate the future, flee from the present, and seek security in the past. The prophets of Israel battled against the pagan deities and priestly cults in the name of the God of hope—*Deus Spes*. Bloch criticized religion as *re-ligio*, in its etymological sense, as a binding back to the past.[25] Messianism is a break with the static myths of creation and their fascination for protological origins. The atmosphere of messianism is history, with its vision of the mystery of the kingdom and the numinous quality of the future.

Bloch demythologizes the eschatological myths of messianic religion by anthropologizing the kingdom and humanizing its picture of God. "Man is the God of Christianity, and anthropology is the secret of Christian theology."[26] This is the meta-religious meaning of the myth of the incarnation, and of the *homoousios* of Jesus with God the Father.[27] True messianism can be achieved only by taking God out of the sky where he has been projected by religion, realizing that at last he stands for the goal of the world, anticipated by hope. Bloch believes in the kingdom—without God; he accepts the contents of the biblical hope—without faith; he looks for the fulfillment of messianism—without a Messiah. "Messianism is older than belief in the Messiah."[28]

Bloch is no stranger to or enemy of religion. He wishes to salvage its eschatological meaning by stripping away its superstitious forms. The basic superstition is the belief in a God-hypostasis, an *ens perfectissimum* above and outside our world. The perfections of reality that are projected in the ideal of God are

[25] *Ibid.*, Vol. I, p. 67.
[26] *Ibid.*, Vol. III, p. 1520.
[27] *Ibid.*, p. 1493.
[28] *Ibid.*, p. 1459.

true as objects of hope, as goals to be realized in the future of a world in process. Thus, the idea of God has a meta-religious significance; its utopian function is its original substratum of meaning. Bloch seeks to rediscover the utopia in religion by taking religion out of utopia. God as the subject is dissolved in the predicates of his kingdom, and his kingdom is future. The God whom traditional religion says already exists as an absolute hypostasis is the destiny of mankind itself. "*Eritis sicut Deus* is the good news of salvation in Christianity."[29] Christology is transformed into utopian anthropology. The classical idea of *Deus absconditus* is an expression of the mystery of *homo absconditus*. The *totaliter aliter* in God, for which Karl Barth contended, is affirmed by Bloch as the hidden, and still-to-be-realized future in man. Bloch is a humanist; his denial of God as an independent existing being is motivated by his interest in the radical humanizing of religion. Like Feuerbach before him, he feels that for man's sake he must "negate the negation of humanity."[30]

III
A SUMMARY OF THEOLOGICAL CRITICISM

A fuller presentation of the whole skeleton of Bloch's philosophy needs to be done in a different setting. We singled out a few points of interest as background for the theological discussion with him. Bloch's atheism has not deterred theologians from welcoming his philosophy as an incentive to renew theology by way of a reappropriation of eschatology. It would be erroneous to speak of a Blochian school in theology, yet his influence on J. B. Metz, W. Pannenberg, J. Moltmann, G. Sauter and W.-D. Marsch is traceable and in some respects considerable. They see that his categories of hope, newness, and the future correspond to the biblical picture of man and history as moving forward in the tension between promise and fulfillment. The arrows in the biblical conception of reality as history are always pointing toward the future. The Word of God is proclaimed always within the hori-

[29] *Ibid.,* p. 1504.
[30] *Ibid.,* p. 1519.

zon of the future, even when it refers back to the exodus in the Old
Testament or back to the cross and resurrection of Jesus in the
New Testament. The prophets and apostles recalled the past to
stir up hope in a God who will do new and better things in the
future. Bloch's philosophy of hope is being hailed as a secular
confirmation of the fact that biblical eschatology deals with what
is central in human existence and vital in historical reality.
Man's hopes burst open his present, connect him with the future
in his past insofar as it is not merely a dead past, and drive him
toward the front-line where the "not-yet" of God's kingdom is
struggling to become an "already"—a permanent, total, universal,
final and perfect realization, in which "God will be all in all."

The theologians we have mentioned are neither uncritical of
Bloch—as our summary of their criticisms will show—nor are
they trying "to elevate him as the Church Father of the
twentieth century."[31] Bloch's philosophy rather has the effect of
animating their minds to a new activation of the unused light and
heat stored in the powerhouse of eschatology in the Bible and the
Christian tradition. Bloch's philosophy also composes a better
agenda for theological discussion than, say, Heidegger's philosophy. As a bridge to the broader cultural currents and to the social and political realities of the twentieth century, Heidegger's philosophy has not done much for theology. Above all, it has
done little to inspire theologians to build their theology in Old
Testament foundations.

James M. Robinson has rightly suggested that Old Testament
scholarship will contribute to a new synthesis of theology only
if it "can relate itself significantly to broader cultural or philosophical currents of the day, in terms of which the Old Testament position could be expressed in the other theological depart-
ments and even outside of theology proper."[32] Then he suggests
that theology enter into a new correlation with the thought of
the later Heidegger, and thus go beyond Bultmannianism with

---

[31] Ernst Bloch, *Religion im Erbe,* ed. by Jürgen Moltmann (Hamburg:
Siebenstern Taschenbuch Verlag, 1967), p. 15.

[32] James M. Robinson, "The Historicality of Biblical Language," ed. by
Bernard W. Anderson, *The Old Testament and Christian Faith* (Harper &
Row, 1963), p. 151.

its attachment to the earlier Heidegger of *Being and Time*. "One must say that Heidegger has in principle (though not in practice) provided the avenue through which Old Testament research may move beyond the confines of its discipline into a central role in theological and philosophical discussion in our day. What is now needed is for biblical scholarship to make use of this opening."[33] There is something half-prophetic in Robinson's statement, only he had the wrong name. What he hoped for from the later Heidegger is not materializing at all, although the shift from the earlier to the later phases of his thinking took place over three decades ago. Bloch's philosophy, on the other hand, has already had the effect of arousing the systematic imagination to unite with Old Testament studies and to reassert a fundamental continuity between the Old and New Testaments in terms of an eschatological interpretation of hope and history, promise and future. The thought of the later Heidegger does achieve a new relation to history, primarily to the history of philosophy and the history of language. However, as Wolfhart Pannenberg has observed, "In the later writings of Heidegger the correlation of being with the future recedes into the background, and the reason for this is perhaps that already in *Being and Time* Heidegger knows of no future beyond death and therefore also no genuine eschatology."[34] Moreover, the dialogue in theology that has been prompted by the later writings of Heidegger has not focused on eschatology as the future of history, but on language as the "house of being."[35] Thus, theology that is informed by the later Heidegger veers toward a mystical sense of language as the locus for the revelation of pure being. It appears that theology becomes unhinged from history whether it be the earlier or the later Heidegger who leads the way. The perspectives which Robinson gains from the later Heidegger, first

[33] *Ibid.*, p. 155.

[34] Wolfhart Pannenberg, "Uber historische und theologische Hermeneutik," *Grundfragen systematischer Theologie* (Göttingen: Vandenhoek & Ruprecht, 1967), p. 147.

[35] See *The Later Heidegger and Theology,* Vol. I of *New Frontiers in Theology,* ed. by James M. Robinson and John B. Cobb, Jr. (Harper & Row, 1963).

in regard to the Old Testament and then systematic theology, are at the opposite pole of a theology that reads the Old Testament from an eschatological perspective, as Bloch's philosophy encourages. According to Robinson, "the wonder that Israel is, rather than not being at all, is the basic experience of Israel in all its history."[36] Is it a credible resume of the Old Testament to state that the core of Israel's historical experience is "the wonder of its being"?[37] From this clue we are led further to the suggestion that the center of theology, and of the Christian faith as well, is the wonder at the fact that things are at all. This means that the age-old ontological question "Why is there something and not nothing?" is elevated as the leading question to which the Bible and theology are to respond. This question was very dear to Tillich, but even he admitted so clearly in *Biblical Religion and the Search for Ultimate Reality* that ontological wonder is not the central motif in the biblical writings. Robinson's positive intention is that "the theological concept of the *Creation of creatures* may gain new relevance. . . . The term *God the Creator,* as a non-metaphysical term, may again become useful in theological discourse."[38] This is, of course, most desirable and urgently needed. But there are two questions. The first is whether wonder and awe in the face of the sheer givenness of things are at the heart of the Old Testament, and not rather hope and trust in the God of exodus whose mode of being is future itself;[39] the second is whether *Deus Creator* must not be interpreted in the light of *Deus Spes,* protology in the light of eschatology, the Alpha in the light of the "End- and Omega-God."[40] If theology is to gain a new perspective on the "ontological dimension of the Christian message,"[41] one would hope that the eschatological core of that mes-

---

[36] J. M. Robinson, "The Historicality of Biblical Language," *op. cit.,* p. 156.

[37] *Ibid.,* pp. 156-157.

[38] *Ibid.,* p. 158.

[39] Ernst Bloch characterizes Jahweh of the Old Testament as a God "mit Futurm als Seinsbeschaffenheit," *Das Prinzip Hoffnung,* Vol. III, p. 1458.

[40] *Ibid.*

[41] J. M. Robinson, "The Historicality of Biblical Language," *op. cit.,* p. 157.

sage would not be smothered by an ontology that goes against its grain.

It is within the context of a theological situation stamped by Heidegger's influence—whether it be his analysis of existence received by the Bultmannians or his ontological hermeneutic of language promoted by the post-Bultmannians—that a number of theologians have arisen to contest this alliance. Their key is eschatology, and Bloch's philosophy helps them to turn it. Wolfhart Pannenberg states: "Perhaps Christian theology will have Ernst Bloch's philosophy of hope to thank if it gains the courage to recover its central category, the full concept of the eschatological. What is decisive in this is the outlook on a future that is to be understood in a temporal sense. Bloch has taught us to understand anew the overwhelming power of the still open future and of the hope which anticipates it, for the life and thought of man as well as for the ontological quality of all reality. He has rediscovered the eschatological way of thinking in the biblical traditions as a theme for philosophical reflection, and also for Christian theology."[42] In similar vein Moltmann states: "As scarcely any other philosophy *Das Prinzip Hoffnung* is suited to help in activating and elaborating the Christian doctrine of hope. . . . *Das Prinzip Hoffnung* can in the present situation of Christian theology give us courage to try a new interpretation of the original Christian hope . . . to free it from the Babylonian captivity into which it has fallen."[43] Wolf-Deiter Marsch makes these statements: "Evangelical Christians can find in him [Bloch] a worthy partner in the discussion so urgently needed today about the basis, content, and goal of Christian hope—a hope in a God who is coming—especially when so many of the leading images of the 'good old order' as well as of an otherworldly fulfillment have become so questionable."[44] And: "The Christian will feel himself much more closely akin to a utopian thinker like Bloch

[42] W. Pannenberg, "Der Gott der Hoffnung," *Grundfragen systematischer Theologie*, p. 390.

[43] J. Moltmann, "Die Kategorie Novum in der christlichen Theologie," *Ernst Bloch zu ehren*, pp. 243-244.

[44] W. -D. Marsch, *Hoffen Worauf?*, pp. 91-92.

than to all those who, filled with anxiety about the present situation, hazard no option at all for the future."[45]

Does this mean that theology is once again going to pay too high a price for a timely alliance with philosophy? There are those who have expressed this fear.[46] The fear, however, is based on a misunderstanding. Bloch's philosophy, as we have said, drives theology to return to its own theme—the full concept of the eschatological. These theologians are rediscovering the fuse which leads to the original explosives in the messianic and missionary religion of the Bible—the confident hope in the God of history and the futurity of his kingdom. On the basis of their rediscovery, they in turn address criticisms to Bloch's philosophy of hope for failing to anchor it in a genuine eschatology.

Gerhard Sauter, in his monumental book on the problem of the future, *Zunkunft und Verheissung,* devoted a major section to Bloch's philosophy. His conclusion is that while Bloch succeeds in maintaining an eschatological perspective with more consistency than most theologians, who usually fall back on a circular view of history *(restitutio in integrum),* after much protesting that they are eluding the snare of Plato's idea of time and eternity, Bloch's own eschatology is trapped in an ontology whose *Logos* deprives both hope of its basis in the Word of promise and the future of its ground in God—instead of the world. "The chief objection that must be raised against Bloch . . . has to be with his *fictive eschatology.*"[47]

What kind of eschatology can be coupled with Bloch's idea of possibility? What is the basis of hope? What is the ultimate ontological ground of the future toward which hope aspires? This is where Pannenberg's brilliant critique of Bloch's idea of the future sets in. Bloch's concern for a real hope and his passion for real newness in the future are scarcely compatible with his

---

[45] *Ibid.,* p. 108.

[46] For example, in quite a few of the reviews collected in *Diskussion über die "Theologie der Hoffnung,"* ed. by W. -D. Marsch (München: Chr. Kaiser Verlag, 1967).

[47] Gerhard Sauter, *Zukunft und Verheissung,* p. 354.

category of possibility (*Objective-real-Mögliche*) which sinks into his concept of the latent tendency or potency in the process of matter.[48] If the future is already inherent in the latent potencies of the world process, or in the hopes and wishes of man, then it loses its ontological priority, its over-against-ness in relation to all past and present reality. It is not Bloch's intention to account for the eschatological symbols, such as hope for the kingdom of God, in a purely psychological sense, as expressions of human wishes. But what other recourse does he have if they can only be referred back to the inner fecundities of matter instead of ahead of us to the future of God? "The primacy of the future," says Pannenberg, "and its newness are only assured if the coming kingdom is ontologically grounded in itself and owes its future not merely to the presently existing wishes and efforts of man. When the coming kingdom is designated in the Bible as the kingdom of *God,* it is concerned to express this ontological primacy of the future of the kingdom over everything that is presently real, including all psychic states. Thus, in fact the being of God and of the kingdom are identical in the Bible, for the being of God is his rulership. . . . This goes to indicate that the thematic of the idea of God is by no means validly and convincingly removed by Bloch, for the question must arise for his own thought how to secure the ontological priority of the coming kingdom before all that exists in the present, also over against men and their most cherished hopes."[49] Bloch's thought is struggling to found hope on the future; his hope is "for a fulfillment coming from an unprecedented and overpowering future."[50] He asserts the primacy of hope in human existence and the priority of the future in historical reality, but both become immersed in a concept of material reality and the historical process which denies them a basis in a genuine eschatology. A genuine eschatology in which the ontological priority of the future is secured is identical with the question of God and his futurity.

Jürgen Moltmann, like Pannenberg, does not believe that Bloch's idea of the future can thrive on the foundations of his

---

[48] W. Pannenberg, "Der Gott der Hoffnung, *op. cit.,* p. 390.

[49] *Ibid.,* p. 391.

[50] *Ibid.,* p. 392.

atheistic humanism. On the other hand, Bloch's zeal for the future, however wobbly its basis, can put to shame the futureless orientation of so much Christian theology. "A dialogue with these humanists who are seeking a 'future without God' can become a suasion to Christians to cease seeking 'God without his future.' In such a meeting of ideologies, the aspect of Christian eschatology which is concerned with this world must be emphasized, for the very purpose of showing the significance of that aspect of Christian hope that transcends this world."[51] Without the transcendence of God, the future's transcendence is mired in the matter of creation. The result of Bloch's demythologization of God, oddly, is his remythologization of nature, transferring to matter what belongs to God. "Clearly, one must ask if it is necessary to pay such a price for the activation of hope in the process of history."[52] Christian hope is based on the power of God's future, not on the inner possibilities of matter. For all these inner possibilities, in the last analysis, break up on the reefs of the negating power of death. Then what? Only faith in a God who can create the *Novum ex nihilo* can found a hope that strives toward a future homeland (*Heimat*) beyond the negativities of the present. That is, only an eschatology that is drawn through the needle's eye of death and resurrection can carry a hope in the face of death itself. Bloch's hope is finally based on the imperishable core of human existence. Something deathless in the individual endures into the future. There is an immortal aspect of man which the future receives into itself.[53] Bloch's doctrine of hope, thus, is not equal to Christian hope, because it tries to cheat death of its due. What is the meaning of the future face to face with death? "Here Marxism is powerless."[54] The Christian faith answers the mortality of death with the promise of new life, based on the death and resurrection of Jesus Christ.

Bloch looks forward to a "happy ending" for all in all. In the struggle of history there is risk and danger; success is not guar-

---

[51] J. Moltmann, "Hope Without Faith: An Eschatological Humanism without God," *Is God Dead?*, *Concilium* 16 (Paulist Press, 1967), p. 28.

[52] *Ibid.*, p. 31.

[53] Ernst Bloch, "Hoffnungsbilder gegen den Tod," *Das Prinzip Hoffnung*, Vol. III, pp. 1297ff.

[54] J. Moltmann, "Hope Without Faith," *op. cit.*, p. 34.

anteed beforehand. In one of Bloch's recent lectures he raised the question, "Can Hope Be Disappointed?" His answer was, "Indeed, otherwise it would not be hope."[55] Yet, with respect to the total and final outcome of history, Bloch is confident. The process itself will not miscarry, only—apparently—some of the steps along the way. W.-D. Marsh asks "Why is there only this end for Bloch— and not nothing-ness?"[56] The title of Marsch's discussion with Bloch poses the question: *Hoffen Worauf?* On what does Bloch place his hope for a total fulfillment in that future home- land of which nothingness is the absolute negation? Can Bloch's philosophy stay indefinitely in the zone of hope, without hope's transcendent basis in the future of God? It is the task of Chris- tian theology, which shares Bloch's pathos for the future, to es- tablish what it means by God and his revelation in Christ in relation to the question of the future of man and his world.

[55] Ernst Bloch, "Kann Hoffnung enttäuscht werden?" in *Verfremdungen V* (Frankfurt: Suhrkamp Verlag, 1962), pp. 211-219.
[56] W. -D. Marsch, *Hoffen Worauf?*, p. 97.

4

God and the Idea
of the Future

Carl E. Braaten

I read this paper to the members and guests of the Senior Common Room at Mansfield College, Oxford University, in the Spring of 1968. Its substance sets forth the web of ideas that I was then spinning out for my book, *The Future of God.* It appeared thereafter in *Dialog,* a journal of theology, Autumn, 1968.

I
BEGINNING AT THE END

In the long run it may become evident that radical theology has been having a cathartic effect on the Church and its theology. The "death of God" phase may have helped to force theology to find a new beginning. Many of us have shared with the radical theologians the experience of the collapse of the going systems. Whether one has come up more through Barth, Bultmann, or Tillich, the feeling is quite general that we can hardly go on the way we have been going. Some have responded to this feeling by dropping out of theology altogether. The symbol of this experience is the exodus from the Church to the world. Others continue to occupy themselves with religious words and objects even when the R.Q. (reality quotient) of such things has fallen to zero. The symbol of this position is the transfer from a chair of theology in a Church seminary to a religion department in a state university. We hope that there is another way, not because we are against moving into the world (we have an address there too) or to a religion department in a state university (some of my best friends teach religion), but because the Church needs more and deserves better than that, and so does the world and the university. It is doubtful that what the world or the university needs most at this time is more "drop-out" Christians and theologians. What is beyond doubt is that the Church needs a new theology, to help give it a renewed sense of the source of power and the goal of mission.

The new place to start in theology is at the end. What Ernst Bloch puts forth as an ontological assertion may be adopted as a theological principle: "The real genesis is not at the beginning, but at the end."[1] Christianity began with the arrival of the future of God's kingdom in the person of Jesus of Nazareth. The rediscovery of the role of eschatology in the preaching of Jesus and of early Christianity has been one of the most important events of recent theological history. The findings of biblical theologians, however, have not always been taken seriously by systematic theologians. The main response of systematic theology to the rediscovery of eschatology was to so redefine the eschatology in question that it lost its futurity. Eschatology was understood as the dimension of the eternal shining through the temporal in rather Platonic fashion. The dialectical theologians without exception took up the problem of eschatology in terms of the qualitative difference between eternity and time, or between the infinite and the finite, while the future of eschatological hope was absorbed into an incarnate word of the past, or into an existential moment in the present.

In our theological youth most of us were nursed on one brand or other of realized eschatology. If there has been an inner-theological move beyond Barth, Bultmann, and Tillich, and not merely a lapse of tired minds and empty hearts into the two-bit versions of secularized theology, it has been prompted by incredulity in face of the exaggerated claims of realized eschatology. Eschatology has never been as realized as Christian propaganda claims. Christianity has been guilty of a lot of false advertising. A realized eschatology in this imperfect world of imperfect men is unbelievable, or it is believable only if the realization that is alleged to have occurred is so interiorized as to make it

---

[1] Ernst Bloch, *Das Prinzip Hoffnung* (Frankfurt: Suhrkamp Verlag, 1959), Vol. III, p. 1628.

irrelevant to the world as it actually is. A realized eschatology is incredible to faithful Jews who remember the wide scope of the promises of God for this world and its future.[2] Christians too, who have been called "honorary Jews," should find the claims of realized eschatology somewhat embarrassing if they have any feel for the enormity of evil that still holds sway in this world. If they really remember the promises of God and pay attention to the legitimate hopes of men, they can only hold an eschatology which reveals the distance between what has already occurred and what has yet to happen before the world reaches its essential home in the fullness of God himself. A theology that begins with eschatology will have to forsake the enthusiasm of realized eschatology, which locates the final fulfillment in the past. I am afraid that the Christian posture evoked by realized eschatology is that of turning one's back to the future, and one's face to the past. If the fulfillment lies in the past, then the preaching of the gospel takes the form of inviting people to return to it. I think it more appropriate, however, to speak with W. Pannenberg and others of a proleptic eschatology, which holds that the Christ-event is a prolepsis, an anticipatory embodiment of the final future of mankind and of the fullness of life through which the glory of God shall manifest itself uninhibitedly in the end. Then the preaching of the gospel, filled with the history of the biblical Christ, is *at the same time* primarily oriented to the future, to the future of Christ who has gone ahead of us by putting death behind himself in the event of his resurrection. I would argue that only a theology which builds man's passion for the future into its very structure can be responsive to the actual human condition. The Christian gospel is relevant to man because it announces the coming of the future for which man as man hopes, that is, the future of identity-in-fulfillment. The first-fruits of this future identity-in-fulfillment have been born already from the grave. To that extent, there is an element of actualization in eschatology. Only in the resurrection of Christ has the future of

[2] See Dorothee Sölle, *Christ the Representative, An Essay in Theology after the "Death of God"* (Fortress Press, 1967), especially the section entitled "The Provisionality of Christ—A Note to the Dialogue with Judaism," pp. 107-112.

life for which men hope been realized on the far side of death. A Christian theology that takes its eschatology seriously has to be a theology formed by the event of Easter.

II
THE SELF-DEFINITION OF GOD

The primary concern of every theology has to be the doctrine of God. The Christian definition of God must arise from his eschatological self-definition in the resurrection of Jesus of Nazareth, as the One "who gives life to the dead and calls into existence the things that do not exist" (Rom. 4:17). The "God-is-dead" theologies provide interesting case studies of what happens to the doctrine of God when theology is de-eschatologized (I mean defuturized) and the resurrection of Jesus is denied. To say that "God is dead" is only a fair description of a theism in which eschatology has faded out. It may well be that the "God" who is dead is but a name which functions for conditions of religious experience and belief that were erroneously thought to be immutable. Henri de Lubac has made the observation, "Every time that mankind abandons a system of thought, it thinks it is losing God."[3] We may be experiencing today birth pangs of a future in which God will establish himself as the power of finalizing fulfillment, the preview of which, the preliminary result of which, we proclaim and celebrate in the raising of Jesus from the dead.

It is not the case, I think, that we have a fairly good idea of God, and then at some later point take up the supplementary problems of eschatology and resurrection. Eschatology and resurrection together make up the medium of our knowledge of God. The "death of God" phenomenon must be taken as a positive sign within Christian theology that natural theology is dead as a way of reaching the identity of God. If we are to speak of God at all, we must speak of him eschatologically as the power of the future which has arrived as the promise of man's fulfillment in the Messiah

[3] Quoted by J. B. Metz, "Zukunft gegen Jenseits?" in *Christentum und Marxismus Heute*, ed. by Erich Kellner (Zürich: Europa Verlag, 1966), p. 223.

Jesus. Jesus of Nazareth is the person in whom the promises of
the God of Israel and the hopes of men for complete and permanent fulfillment are united. Where there is life, there is hope,
and where there is hope, there is religion,[4] and where religion
receives the promise of God for the fulfillment of life through the
person of Jesus, there is Christianity.

If Christian language of God is to ring true today, it must
happen at the point of man's quest for fulfillment, at the point
where the hopes of men converge on the question of the ultimate
future. If it is irrelevant for man to use the language of hope and
to be in quest of fulfillment beyond the horizon of what has been
and the present state of affairs, then it is irrelevant to speak
of God. Natural theology is dead as a way of establishing the
identity of God; it is not dead, but essential, as a way of describing the human situation within which the question of God does
arise. Natural theology can take the form of a phenomenology of
hope in human existence. It can be even more broadly developed
as a phenomenological description of the proleptic structure of
all language and reality, of all history and existence, as though
echoing Paul's cry about the whole creation waiting with eager
longing and groaning in travail until now, when the revelation
of their end and fulfillment in the magnificent future of God has
taken place in the resurrection of Jesus and the effusion of the
Spirit. Of course, this is not a neutral phenomenology which proceeds unconsciously as though the anticipatory structure of all
reality and experience had not already been revealed as such by
God's eschatological self-definition in Jesus of Nazareth. It is a
critical phenomenology, one which views the phenomena within
the horizon of the future that has arrived in the Christ-event.

If the identity of God cannot be established by way of natural
theology or by the history of religions, the Christian has no other
recourse but to start with the eschatological self-definition of God
in Jesus of Nazareth. God has given himself an identity for man
in the form of a man. Jesus represents God to us. He alone can
show us the Father. Jesus is not a substitute for God, as though
in having Jesus we have no need for God. The "God is dead" the-

---

[4] Ernst Bloch, *Das Prinzip Hoffnung*, Vol. III, p. 1404.

ology is Jesuological in the extreme. It takes Jesus as a substitute for God, quoting its favorite verse from John, "He that hath seen me hath seen the Father" (John 14:9). However, it is the essence of heathenism to make substitutes for God. If Jesus stands in for God, eclipsing the One he is supposed to reveal, we have fallen back into a form of heathenism. It was the whole burden of the ancient struggle over the Trinity to prevent Christianity from such a lapse of faith.

If we wish to refer our hopes to Jesus, we must see how he referred them to the approaching kingdom of God. It was not like Jesus to draw attention to himself for his own sake. The claims he made about himself were entirely based on the authority of the coming future of God's rule. Jesus can define God for us, only because he first let himself be defined wholly by the absolute future of God's kingdom. If we delete the reference to God and his kingdom in the appearance of Jesus, there is nothing left in Jesus to which we can refer our own hopes. And if Jesus can no longer define and mobilize our hopes, he is irrelevant to our future. Then "Jesus" becomes an empty name, in no way exalted above all others.

III
THE POWER OF THE FUTURE

Jesus defined God for us in terms of the imminent future of his kingdom. Jesus' God was Jahweh. He knew God in terms of the promises that had been given to Israel. He packed the promises and the hopes of Israel into his preaching of the kingdom. The kingdom of God was "the power of the future" pressing in upon him, and through him upon his hearers. Here we take up the symbol of "the power of the future" as a modern translation of "the kingdom of God." Kingdom-talk is quite alien in a culture which has dethroned its kings. Lords and kings do not impress us anymore. So we need a shift of symbolism away from this cultural anachronism. But may we not capture the meaning of the "kingdom of God" by speaking of the power of the future? The future is a mystery. It comes, as God's kingdom comes, *en dun-*

amei—in power. Jesus anticipated the power of God from the future.

In late Judaism and in the New Testament the word "God" was often replaced by "heaven." The kingdom of God and the kingdom of heaven meant the same thing. Power was something that came into the world from heaven above. But "heaven" for us today is a poor equivalent for "God." As an expression of transcendence, it no longer irradiates much meaning. For many of us the heavens are not filled with the mystery and majesty of God, and we do not expect deliverance from above. We may instead think of the power of deliverance as arriving from the future. God as the power of the future comes to us from ahead. In this way we can try to give expression to the futurity of Jesus' own expectation of the kingdom of God.

On the basis of Jesus' preaching of the kingdom, we may try to re-eschatologize our symbols of God. The Platonic essences, the Stoic logos, and the Hellenistic world-scheme in general succeeded in bringing about a massive shift away from an historico-eschatological framework of thought to that of a mystical ontology. As someone has said, it was not long before Christianity became a kind of Platonism to the masses. If we now try to bend the framework of thought to adjust to a future-oriented conception of reality as historical movement in which man is a child of promise, driven toward the future by the dynamic of hope, we may try to think of God with futurity as essential to his very being.[5] The being of God is his eschatological power. When Jesus said, "Seek ye first the kingdom of God," he fused the reality of God's kingdom into his very being. Jesus could not appeal for ultimate commitment to the kingdom unless God were thought to be identical with his kingdom.[6] The promises of the kingdom are identical with God in the state of their ultimate fulfillment. The living God of the Bible experiences in himself the tension between promise and fulfillment. There is a dimension of the "not-yet" in God him-

[5] In describing Israel's picture of Jahweh, Ernst Bloch speaks of a God "mit Futurum als Seinsbeschaffenheit": *Das Prinzip Hoffnung*, Vol. III, p. 1458.

[6] See Wolfhart Pannenberg, "Der Gott der Hoffnung," *Grundfragen systematischer Theologie* (Göttingen: Vandenhoek & Ruprecht, 1967), p. 393.

self. He is not a stationary deity, who in every sense is already all that he will be in the finality and purity of his Spirit. If God is identical with his Word, and his Word reaches us in the form of promise that has not yet been fulfilled, we may draw the implication that there is something in God himself that corresponds to this state of unfulfillment. God is the reality of his Word, first in the form of historical promise, and finally in the spiritual form of fulfillment. However, when the dominant notion of the Word was determined by the apophantic Logos of Stoic and Platonic philosophy, the dynamic, creative, and history-oriented character of the Word of promise was obscured. The result was a Hellenized view of the eternity, infinity, and immutability of God, which could not allow for a tension in God between the history of promise and the eschatological future of fulfillment. If God is *homoousios* with his Word, this involves an eschatological unity between the content of the Word and the author.[7] Thus, the Word should not be misunderstood as an eternal self-manifestation of a fixed diety, but as the Word of promise from which a future fulfillment is anticipated. There inheres in the author of the Word of promise the power to generate through history the intended fulfillment. In this unity of the divine mode of being as promise in history and the divine mode of being as eschatological fulfillment, there lies the root of an eschatological conception of the Trinity. And who knows but that then Sabellius' way of thinking might to some extent be rehabilitated?

We have emphasized that in the preaching of Jesus the power that determined all reality was awaited from the future of God's coming kingdom. The power of the coming future pressed for an unconditional obedience, radical receptivity to the conditions of eschatological existence and, above all, freedom from bondage to the past. "No one who puts his hand to the plow and looks back [as we always tend to do in the Church in order to be justified by a thousand safe precedents] is fit for the kingdom of God" (Luke 9:62). The kingdom comes to those who are not satisfied with the past or with the status quo, but are eager and hungry for new things, who look to the hills of God's future for their

---

[7] *Ibid.*, p. 397.

redemption. Jesus could call upon men to relate to himself as to their very future because in him the future became present without ceasing to be ultimate. Here we have the root of the idea of the incarnation, cast in terms of the proleptic presence of the absolute future, rather than in terms of a metamorphosis of a higher being into a lower being. The rule of God's power was present in Jesus through advance symptoms of its futurity.

Jesus did not go before his hearers with the information that there was such a thing as the kingdom of God. That would not have been to tell them anything new. Rather, he announced that the rule of God was drawing so near that its impact was already being impressed upon them through him. The eschatological day is dawning; its glimmerings are already breaking out in Jesus' works and words. It involves judgment. A person will be judged by his attitude to Jesus who is the fulcrum of the future, the place where the old is phasing out to make room for the new. To decide for Jesus is to be open to the future of God. Disciples of Jesus become partisans of the future, advocates of freedom and forerunners of newness. For to be free is to have a future. To believe in Jesus is to let him keep our future open for new things which the power of the future aims to release into our present. A person will be justified, therefore, through his relation to Jesus, if Jesus' claim to be the advance agent of the kingdom of God, that is, his claim to authority, is not mistaken. The justification of sinners and the godless is linked to the eschatological judgment already proleptically enacted in Jesus' ministry. The Messiah Jesus is the believer's hope because through faith in him he, so to speak, pockets in advance a merciful verdict. He lives already now from the end, by the anticipatory power of hope. That is how I think one must locate the logic of the forgiveness of sins as an eschatological event of grace.

IV
THE RESURRECTION AS THE KEY

The eruption of the power of the future in the ministry of Jesus constitutes a real presence and union of God with him. This is a confession of the Godhood of Jesus that can only be made, as in fact it first came to be made, retrospectively in the light of Easter. None of Jesus' contemporaries called him God. An event that lay in the future of Jesus himself could alone certify his ministry as a unique act of God, by which the swaying power of the eschatological future identified itself with the history of Jesus. This event that had retroactive power to grasp the ministry of Jesus as the authentic sacrament of the ultimate future of mankind was the resurrection.

Christian hope is based on the resurrection of Jesus of Nazareth because through it God defined himself as the power of the living future beyond the finality of death. In the resurrection God identified himself with the cause of Jesus and promised to give it a future beyond death. The cause of Jesus could be continued in history. This cause was spelled out in Jesus' ministry by his bringing eschatological foretokens of salvation to the poor and the paralyzed, to the sick and the blind, to outcasts and sinners. But what he brought was at best a foretaste of something more; it was only a sample of the fulfillment of life which the present was incapable of securing. Even the present that was then qualified by being with Jesus was not sufficient of itself. And the same is true for Christians now. The present that is qualified by being in Christ is not the end and should not be confused with the ecstasy of fulfillment. The pilgrimage is still underway, and the goal is still out in front. What did Paul say? "Not that I have already obtained this or am already perfect; but I press on to make it my own, because Christ Jesus has made me his own. Brethren, I do not consider that I have made it my own, but one thing I do; forgetting what lies behind and straining forward to what lies ahead, I press on toward the goal. . . ." (Phil. 3:12-14).

Two things are of crucial importance in the resurrection of Jesus, the fact that it happened in history and its eschatological significance for the whole of mankind. Nothing is more fatal to the Christian faith than to locate the meaning of the resurrection outside its happening. The meaning must be inherent in the event, and read out of it, or, I think, we must admit that Christianity is a desperately uninteresting affair. Christian faith, so far as it can be distinguished from other structures of religious belief, is a confession to the One who raised Jesus from the dead. If God is stripped of this means of his self-identification, we can only count ourselves among those who have lost their hope, or who have exchanged the Christian hope for some other one. Then we must fall silent about God, or speak of some idol in lieu of God, for the meaning of the name of the Christian God is defined by the revelation of his creative power to give life to the dead and to bring into existence things that do not exist. If we want to say that the meaning of a word is its function, then the meaning of "God" is his function. The function we have in mind is not to lend prestige to traditional Christian values or ideals, as Paul van Buren's "God," whom he calls the "imaginary ideal observer," is reduced to doing; rather, the function and, therefore, the meaning of the God who reveals himself in the Christ-event are exhibited in the event which the earliest Christians unanimously called a resurrection. What I am saying is that if we do not define God in the language of the resurrection hope, the basis of a truly eschatological mode of God-talk has been removed. According to Paul, the best we can have apart from the God who raised Jesus from the dead is the God of wrath (1 Thess. 1:10). Or perhaps we could at best match the God-forsaken cry of Jesus from the cross, which is a cry of hopelessness and futurelessness. This is why I said that "the God is dead" theology is a consistent result of a defuturized eschatology and of the denial of the resurrection of Jesus as an event of history. To speak of God within the horizon of man's hope for the future of identity-in-fulfillment is to speak of what God has done to Jesus by advancing him into the future of life beyond life's eschaton of death. The resurrection of Jesus offers to mankind a new eschaton that puts death to death.

We have been saying that the dimensions of the eschatological future as man's horizon of hope and the event of Jesus' resurrection as God's self-identification constitute the conditions for a renewal of a vital speaking of God in our day. It seems to us that there must still be some way of defining what is essentially Christian. We do not use the word "Christian" evaluatively but only descriptively. It might, after all, be better to be a Buddhist. There is an element of tyranny in the position that makes it impossible to know by what act of unbelief one might succeed in ceasing to be in fact a Christian. Christians should make it possible for an honest man to quit being a Christian. To do this charitably they must not stretch the definition of what it means to be a Christian so broadly that it embraces each step of conscious disavowal of the specific contents of the Christian faith. It seems to me that most of the talk about "anonymous Christianity"[8] adds up to a kind of imperialism which says that no matter what you don't believe, we Christians are going to insist on claiming you for our side. If I have focused my thoughts about God and Jesus so exclusively on the kingdom and on resurrection, it is because any new translation of the Christian faith for our time must find at those focal points the norms of faith, the objects of hope, and the energies of love.

[8] Karl Rahner's idea of "anonymous Christianity" seems to me to be a very questionable theologoumenon, echoing a 19th-century Protestant notion, advanced by Richard Rothe, of an "unconscious Christianity" (*unbewusstes Christentum*). That idea came to no good, since it not only downplays the reality of unbelief, but also downgrades the particularity of Christian faith. Christian faith is not a diffuse attitude possessed by all men of good will. Both ideas—of "anonymous Christianity" and of "unconscious Christianity" —seem to build an ethical rather than an eschatological bridge to the universal validity of the Christian claim. See Karl Rahner, "Christianity and the Non-Christian Religions," *Theological Investigations* (Helicon Press, 1966), Vol. V, pp. 115-134.

PART II

Political Eschatology

5

Eschatological Politics and Political Eschatology

Robert W. Jenson

When this piece appeared in *Dialog,* and I reread it with a subscriber's eye, I saw that it was less an essay than the outline of a short book. The compression with which the theme has presented itself to me, and the abstract tenacity of some of the arguments, suggest the contemporary urgency and difficulty of its matter. One has to argue his way from scratch; for although there has been much talk about "political theology," hardly any has actually been done. Perhaps the book will get written some day; but I could not wait, and meanwhile any who find the matter worth the trouble will have to read with attention to the piece's schematic character. The key sections on options for relating ultimate hope to penultimate hopes go back to a lecture given to Lutheran World Federation pastors' conferences in East and West Berlin in the summer of 1968. An important filiation within theology's current problematic is tipped by the assigned subject of that lecture: "The Relation of the Old and New Testaments as a Theological Problem."

Politics is eschatological; eschatology ought to be political. This maxim will already seem a truism, so rapidly has the theological mood which affirms secularization coalesced with the theological program of setting the meaning of theological statements by pointing to a final future. The maxim is already in danger of being handled as an empty tautology: politics is eschatology; eschatology is politics. I associated myself with the maxim before it was a fad, and will stick to it—but only because I think it can be non-vacuously developed. One way of avoiding vacuity would be to remind ourselves that eschatology is not *only* politics: that there can and must be cosmological and aesthetic eschatologies as well. But that will not be our task here.

I

To the first half of the maxim, it is no objection that politics has been practiced in societies that never heard the biblical proclamation of hope. For if that proclamation is indeed *true*, there could be no society whose religion wholly lacked an eschatological component. And it is a fact that those societies that have most nearly suppressed their own eschatological disquiet have also suppressed politics below ideological consciousness. Politics is eschatological because it deals with hopes, if only to manipulate live hopes in the service of past hopes safely dead. Politics is a society's hoping as an activity and a process.

But need hope itself be eschatological? Not, anyway, in the sense that one might want to hope for penultimate futures, e.g., peace or righteousness, but not be able to do this without also buying a final future, that is, God. This would be just a new version of the "God in the gaps": here are a, b, c, d . . . n to hope for in life, and b and d you can't hope for unless you also believe in God. Merely relocating the gaps to be filled under the category "hopes" will not rehabilitate this preternatural God, supposing he was ever habilitated. We will encounter on our way no future possibilities which we can take up only by appealing to God.

But that life is a *way* on which we encounter possibilities is itself an *interpretation;* making this interpretation and believing in God are the same. There are no God-linked hopes. But hoping itself is confession of God. *How* one hopes is confession of *which* God one confesses.

Nor do we thereby set up hope itself as one among other human potentialities and as the gap which only God can fill: it is not that one might wish to hope and not be able to because one did not believe in God. For hope is reflexively omnivorous: to wish to hope is in fact to hope, and so also to believe in God. One can refrain from hoping only by interpreting the world altogether otherwise than as possibility—in which case neither the question of particular hopes nor the question of God arises. Thus there is no question of "having" to hope in God in order to hope politically or otherwise. If one does not hope, one sees no object of hope; and this is not a privation, for it could be a privation only within the interpretation of the world as occasion of hope. We will encounter nothing on our way with which we need God to deal; but we need God to be on a way. If we have no God, and so are not on a way, we do not lack something; we simply live otherwise. Whether this mode of existence is in fact possible is another question.

II

Of course it is not that simple. Here is the complication: Is God himself a particular *object* of hope? Do we have something particular to hope for at the End, and so from God alone? If God is not a special object of hope, as our discussion so far might suggest he is not, then talk of God is syntactical metalinguistic description, in the material mode, of our talk of other objects of hope, and probably now best dispensed with. If he is, then there seems to be a particular hope which, tautologously, is God-linked; and however we set up the relation between this hope and our other hopes, we seem back with God-in-the-hope-gaps.

Indeed, do not our hopes on the way and a hope at the End inevitably cancel each other? If we hope for pie in the sky, can we ever really look for potatoes on earth? And vice versa? Is not a particular eschatological hope the necessary enemy of political hopes? Thus, regularly we see people led by hope in God to commit themselves to political hopes, like the Christians who gave themselves to the Mississippi project and other civil rights enterprises, only to discover that in proportion as these hopes occupy their lives, their need of the being they had called God diminishes. It is sad but true that specific gospel proclamation is usually nearly absent from the communication of exactly those congregations most involved in community action and the like, so that a visit to the *worship* of these with-it congregations is often dreary and stale. Vice versa, the political inaction and stupidity of congregations who talk most of God's final reward in Christ is notorious.

I think the difficulty is solvable, or rather solved, by the gospel. I think also that seeing how the difficulty is solved will show *that* and, more important, *how* politics is eschatological. We will examine the possible schemes.

We can eliminate one scheme immediately: that there are earthly hopes and a heavenly hope, and that they simply succeed each other. For the eschatological hope must be hope *for* all other hopes, or it is not eschatological. This refutation is emptily tautological, but just so appropriate to a vapid suggestion.

Another undialectical proposal, but a serious one, would make the eschatological hope the limit of an infinite series of reinterpretations of political hopes. Just so the Old Testament is the result of a thousand years of repetition of the event that a failed—or achieved—temporal hope was recognized in its ambiguity and partiality, and taken up into a new and whole hope—which again was antiquated and transcended in its time.

Thus the "land" was first Canaan, then Jerusalem, then a land raised above the mountains and inhabited by men with the law written in their hearts. So now it would be our task to find the interpretations of the "land" or of "righteousness" which could be born of the antiquation of older interpretations—as those, to continue the series, in post-exilic Israel, the Constantinian Church or the social gospel—and of the peculiar needs and possibilities of our times as we can see them.

Such hopes would be eschatological because we would know that the fulfillment of our hope for, e.g., social justice as we understand it, would occur precisely in that it was overtaken by a new interpretation thereof. That we thus knew about the process of interpretation and reinterpretation would be our difference from Israel. An end to the series of reinterpretations would not necessarily be expected, for even without it we would have, as the content of our politics in any one epoch of the history of reinterpretation, concrete hopes not surpassable by us.

It is so that eschatological politics are done today. I wish partly to affirm this way, and will return to it later. But there is a problem in this scheme: death is given only ontic, and not ontological significance. And this will not finally do, for the future is after all not only the time for hope. It is also the time of death, which will interpret all hopes so: "It might have been." Israel knew this, and spoke her knowledge without illusion. But she never did anything theological about it. She never gave Jahweh anything to do with death, or death anything to do with Jahweh: she never gave death ontological status. Her choice was right, for in advance of death the only mediation of hope and death is compromise, such as all other ancient cultures made—the alternative would be to be past death, like the New Testament Lord is claimed to be. But thus death remained in Israel a "remarkable theological vacuum,"[1] and the future only ambiguously occupied by hope. This is why Israel was never able to carry the desacralizing of her world through to the end;[2] she needed an open retreat into cultic repetition of a healing *past* origin. It is why Israel was essentially liable to exchange her faith for a *religion* of "law." We have to take the step Israel did not, and confront death and hope in the question with which Israel ended: "Can these bones live?"

One way of taking that step, and preserving hope in the face of death, would be to eternalize hope, to fall back altogether on the manna of religion hoarded by Israel, and make faith altogether into a normal religion. We might envision our hopes always already realized in a timeless ground of being where there could be no death and no threat of the future because there is no not-yet, because there all already is all that it will be. Precisely the failure of our temporal hopes would be the entry to this timeless Being—and death would be the gateway to heaven. Eternalizing hope has been the standard move of the Christian religion.

"Dialectical" theology transcendentalized instead, and made a variant which is the inevitable last stage of the Christian reception of religion and its timeless Being. Specific political or other hopes serve in dialectical theology only to open hoping itself as a mode of existence. What is to be hoped for is not this or that,

[1] Gerhard von Rad, *Theologie des alten Testaments*, II, pp. 371f.
[2] *Ibid.*, p. 366.

but the grace of receiving life as promise. Such hope is immune to death and everything else, for it has no content to be frustrated. Indeed, this sort of hope arises exactly when the knowledge of death removes the content of our hopes. It arises in the crisis of the past in the present moment of futurity, in a judgment upon all concrete contents of the present from a future which itself can never become past because it has no content.

Eternalizing and transcendentalizing our hopes are perfectly feasible ways of rhyming them with death. Together they are the way mankind has universally chosen, and seems likely to choose now. But they are also the depoliticizing of our hopes. For politics takes *time*.

So: political hopes in evasion of death, or ontological recognition of death by depoliticizing hope. What we need is a way to transcend the alternative, and Paul proposed one. He proposed *love* as the solution to this antimony of hope. Love is a concrete content of hope: one can very well say he has loved and give evidence for the assertion; therefore, one can hope to *achieve* love and be able to describe what one hopes for. Yet if we hope for love, we hope in precisely such a way that shipwrecked hope will but beget new hope, hope in a way which cannot be frustrated—even by death. For when I love, I await my life from whatever the loved one does, without wishing to bind in advance what that may be. I expect to *learn* what is good from what the other in fact does. Love is thus at once concrete and transcendent; it is a concrete final hope which does not cancel penultimate hopes, and a transcendent hope which does not lack temporal reality.

But this is too abstract. There is no such thing as "love," only particular loves. Dropping, therefore, the generalities: Jesus of Nazareth gave himself up to our hopes, and interpreted his destiny for himself and us on the shipwreck of those hopes in death. That is to say, he loved us. It is also claimed that he rose again. That is to say, he *succeeded* at love. If I give myself up for the other, and therefore cease myself to exist, I frustrate the gift. Only if I give myself up for the other, and just in this death am the future of the other, do I succeed at love. Only death and resurrection could be successful love. The word of the New Testament promises Jesus' successful love as what we may finally hope for, as the last interpretation of Israel's promises. The dialectics of this promise—and only those of this promise—give us an object of hope which is also the transcendent possibility of hope, a hope which is neither timeless nor transcendental, yet transcendent to every present.

Called to hope for this final object of hope, we can hope in death without either abandoning or detemporalizing our hopes. We can work hopefully for the "land" or for "righteousness" as we understand them, knowing that if we break on our hopes, the land and righteousness will rise up again. For love, the futurity of death, is hope rising again.

Our dying hopes will first rise, we may hope, in ever new interpretation of what we hoped for—as out of the dying hope of integration of America's blacks into white culture there is rising the hope for a new American culture jointly created by independently powerful partial cultures. Thus we return to the standard position of eschatological politics—but with this difference: the new interpretation in which broken hope will live again is not something *we* must bring forth, nor is it demanded by that great abstraction, "history." Rather, if we hope for love as the End, we may expect that a new grasp of the "land" or "righteousness" will be called out of every new catastrophe by the word about Jesus that promises that love. This word can be spoken again after every catastrophe, for it has its own content independent of other contents of hope and, therefore, able always to survive them. Yet when it is spoken it is the possibility of all hopes. It is not a word adventitious to our penultimate hopes: for it is a narrative, and *what* is narrated is the crucifixion of Jesus, the death of our hopes—but now narrated as future.

Or, translating back to the terms of the question with which we began, the final future whose possibility is God is indeed a particular hope. Jesus' love is the final hope. Therefore God, as the reality of this possibility, is an *object* of hope. Yet this hope is not for pie in the sky; it is hope for the resurrection of our potato-hopes.

III

Yet this cannot be the whole story. For if the Christian promise really has a particular independent content, it must also promise a particular time of its fulfillment. Religion's heaven can survive as noplace, but faith's new heaven and earth must be sometime. Otherwise, as we have seen, we must either ignore death, or eternalize or transcendentalize our hopes. To understand the Christian hope, we must speak of *the* final future as a time of its own. Refusal to do this was the fault of dialectical theology—its only fault, but one which drove it to otherworldliness despite its own primary intention.

So we come to the other side of the maxim: eschatology is and ought to be political. We have to describe a last object of hope; and if that object is to be the resurrection of our politics, it must itself be describable in political terms. The Christian promise must be interpretable as describing a last society for which we may hope.

What may we await? We may await *a revolution done by Jesus' undefeatable availability to his fellows, and a consequent new society organized by that love.* Perhaps this hope is preposterous: those who find it so will have to consider for themselves whether or how they will sustain other hopes. Our present task is merely to try to understand it. To that end, we discuss four aspects of the above proposition (A-D below) and enter one disclaimer (E).

A

This hope is hope for a free future action of Jesus, a man once made past by death. It is, therefore, hope in his resurrection. The chief difference between a dead man and a live one is that the live man can still surprise us.

Every dead man is in a certain sense alive, if his achievement shaped the tradition which mediates my present possibilities. I can very well await a future shaped by Socrates, Napoleon or Malcolm X. Indeed, I must. But despite "living on" so, these worthies are dead, for they cannot *surprise* us; their life in the tradition is a *given,* a deposit. If 1 am surprised by Socrates, it is because of my previous ignorance of the tradition, or because someone else has surprised me in connection with the tradition. This sort of aliveness and determination of the future will not do for Jesus—for the future we await from him is successful love, and freedom to surprise is of the essence of love. We await, therefore, that "this same Jesus" will surprise us again out of love.

But what can it mean to say that "this same" anybody will do thus-and-so, when the anybody is one who has died? The question is about the criterion for the use of "same person." Here I will merely state and use that which to me seems appropriate to faith's grasp of reality, without arguing for or defending it— since I have done that elsewhere.[3] In a case where our first criteria of personal identity—in terms of appearance, known location in time and space, etc.—came in conflict with each other, we should mean by personal identity *dramatic continuity* and judge it by *dramatic appropriateness.* We regularly make such judgments, as when we say that scene three did or didn't fit the rest, or that such-and-such an act "had to be" done by Jones, being just what we "should have expected" from him. So, the content of the gospel message, "He is risen," is: we may await unpredictable events recognizable when they occur to be dramatically appropriate as the conclusion of Jesus' life of self-giving—and recognizable as the dramatically appropriate conclusion of our stories as well. In political terms: we may await a revolution dramatically recognizable as a new free act of Jesus, and a consequent new society dramatically recognizable as the conclusion of his life. This stipulation is sufficient in itself, but it does raise metaphysical issues we cannot treat here—see (E) below.

B

In any period of the gospel's history of interpretation, the hope for Jesus' love concretizes itself by drawing to itself the

[3] Robert W. Jenson, *The Knowledge of Things Hoped For* (Oxford University Press, 1969), pp. 150-153.

dreams of the time. Whether these dreams have themselves been influenced by the gospel hope, or are purely "natural," makes no difference here. Such a vision of the last future can and will be mythologically or ideologically elaborated to whatever extent is appropriate to its particular character.

Politically, such a vision of the last future has a *utopian* function, like a platonic idea but on a temporal horizon: it is an unachievable but endlessly approachable limit of political endeavor. There is no politician so pragmatic that he wholly lacks a utopia, even if it be merely the utopia of his own unchallenged rule. And that the man with noble goals is "hard-headedly" aware those goals will never be wholly realized, and that to partially realize them endless compromise will be required, means only that he knows his utopia is one.

Believing utopias differ from others in this: it belongs to their *content* that the believer knows his dream will be broken—he knows about death and gives it ontological significance, but does not therefore despair. For part of what he hopes is just that the death of his dream will be the occasion of Jesus' story calling forth yet a better dream. He does not know what the gospel's new interpretation of the future will be; for that statement of faith's hope which is independent of all utopias, that we "await the conclusion of Jesus' love," is not itself utopian and does not therefore enable predictions of what new utopias it will call to its future interpretation.

So also, our formulation of faith's hope in terms of revolution and a new society is itself already utopian, though minimally so. It draws on the fad-words of the age, and will be transcended. This does not mean it is an as-if sort of thing. If the Christian promises are fulfilled, we will see that just this prediction has been fulfilled—but many other versions of our hope as well.

C

The most obvious thing about "revolution" is that there has never been one—not as the word is used ideologically. Nor will there be—until the gospel's promise is fulfilled. There have been and perhaps will be governmental and social upsets in plenty, while whole civilizations rise and fall, but none of these upsets has been nor will be what a Marx or a Fanon means by "revolution." "Revolution" is an intrinsically eschatological concept.

When S.D.S. types or Paris student revolutionaries are interviewed about their goals, they invariably frustrate their liberal interviewers by insisting the present "system" must be overthrown, but having no intelligible proposals about what should replace it—and by not even being bothered by their lack of proposals. Just thereby they show themselves true revolutionaries. For political description of the revolutionary goal would have to be operational, it would have to specify how to bring it about. And this would mean indicating structures of the existing system to be used as levers on other structures, i.e., to remain themselves intact. At this point we would be back with reform—even if by coercive methods—which is what the liberal interviewers want, but is exactly what the rebels are fed up with. It has always been so: consider the vacuity of Marx's description of the communist society against the rich operational detail of his analyses of capitalist society. What revolutionaries do have, instead of operational proposals, are utopias—but utopias themselves do not need to be brought to pass, and revolutionaries want to bring something to pass.

Thus consistent revolutionaries, such as Mao, have been driven to make revolution its own goal, to proclaim "continuous revolution"—in not at all accidental correspondence to dialectical theology's hope for hoping. Of course, revolt for the sake of revolt is—unless it is nihilistic or merely adolescently suicidal—as nonsensical as hope for the sake of hope. Maoism, like the early Barth, is a titantic and decisively instructive dead-end.

The only one who could make a revolution would be one who lived freedom from the established structures to its fulfilled end, without giving up on the historical human reality mediated in those structures. That is, only he could make a revolution who had freely abandoned his life, who had freely *died,* and who had died of his total acceptance of his fellows in all their hate and alienation. There will only be a revolution if it is made by a loving one who has died. Those of us who say Jesus of Nazareth

is risen say there is such a man, and await the revolution from
him.

Therefore also we can invest revolutionary passion in utopias
known to be utopias, without despair or fanaticism. He will
make the revolution and not we. Just therefore we are free from
ourselves to attack each new status quo with abandon, in the name
of that future which is the meaning of all presents.

D

Likewise, the hope for a new society is not—except in the
rhetoric of a Lyndon Johnson or Richard Nixon—merely the hope
for a society different from, and by some scale of value better
than this one. It is hope for the overcoming of something inherently "old" in all past and present societies and in all future
societies operationally extrapolatable from past or present societies. Our societies are qualitatively old because they live by the
past: their continuity is the same as their persistence, their sta-
bility as their stasis, their existence as the preservation of some
status quo. This is why revolutionaries invariably become conservative as soon as they get power; there is nothing else for those
responsible for a society's existence to do except conserve it.
There are, after all, only two ways of having life: losing it in
order to find it, or hanging on. A *society* which did the first
would indeed be something new.

So the flower children who set out to be a society of *love,* of
mutual self-surrender, indeed conceived the only possible new
society. Their only problem was that non-eschatological societies
cannot love, as their elders tried legalistically and therefore vainly
to warn them. Therefore they were driven, like many other serious monks before them, to primitivism, to the attempt to be as
little a society as possible: to nudity, sexual nihilism, vagabond-
age, anti-rational use of drugs, and the abandonment of language.

That our existence is social means that each of us is himself
only in his place in an identifiable entity not coextensive with him-

self but rather including other selves in their places. I am myself and yet free from myself, that is, am personal, only in that I am something *for you;* and this something is a function assigned neither by you only nor by me only. So we have the perennially observed dialectic of social existence: it at once is the possibility and reality of free life for another, and threatens that freedom by making us mere functions.

The problem is the problem of the center, of what joins you and me to be a unit other than either of us, within which each of us has a function for the other. If we are centered merely by a system or ideal, our society will be qualitatively old, and will reduce us to functions, for systems and ideals cannot love. Therefore societies have regularly sought a *person,* a being who can love, as the center: the King, the Führer, the *theios aner* of a state cult. But those who love and therefore die, and do not *rise* again, fail at love—so that all societies so centered are at last distorted by the frenzied attempts of their centering persons to be immortal.

A "new" society could only be a society centered on one who has loved his fellows unto death and risen from it. This is the gospel's political eschatology: we may await a society ruled by one who gives himself to each of us just *as* each is defined by his past, and in which the function of each of us for the others is defined by the particular sort of *acceptance* which his particular past imposes on the Ruler. I will be for you a particular possibility of love, of free self-giving, a possibility defined in its particularity by the unique past which defines "I". The effective social goal of this society will therefore be God, the Transcendence of the futurity of love.

E

Finally, the problem which I mention here only to indicate I have not forgotten it: the participation in the end-society of those who shall have died. This participation must be affirmed, but the wrench which an eschatology with content gives to our notions of time and personal identity means that this participation, like all the rest of theology, must be rethought. There is, however, no space for that rethinking here: it will involve an entire new metaphysics. If anyone suspects me of using this excuse to postpone a hard task, he is correct.

6

On Becoming Man:
Some Aspects

Robert W. Jenson

This was my "inaugural lecture" at Gettysburg Seminary and appeared in the bulletin of that institution; it reflects both the situation of a one-time lecture to one's regular students and colleagues, and some then-current discussions at that school. The structure which the "dogmatic considerations" of the first part assert for the nexus person-word-future reflects quite closely my theology at that time and the pressures which led me to it. The subsequent explications in terms of "reason" and "organization" are the goal of the piece, and contain whatever is new in it. In general, my contributions to this volume reflect my concern to see how such positions as those summarized in Part I of this essay work out as hermeneutical guides in a wide range of reflection.

This piece will have two main parts. The first will be a condensed statement of some dogmatic considerations, and will begin with two highly arguable but here unargued axioms.

I

Axiom I: Man comes to exist in and out of the world of animals and plants and galaxies precisely when he realizes that he does not yet exist; men are those of God's creatures who have their own true selves not as possessions but as challenges. My humanity is not a set of characteristics which I may be counted on to exemplify: like being vertebrate or brown-haired or sapient. My humanity is rather something that happens, and happens exactly as the event of choice and action in which I become something that I was not before. This axiom is a set of platitudes of

contemporary philosophical and theological anthropology—
but platitudes the consequences of which we have hardly exhausted.

Axiom II: That I am not yet myself and must become it, is
after all something I cannot very well say to myself. Where would
I get the location from which to say it? If I am to discover this
peculiar sort of fact, if I am to discover that my selfhood is an
opportunity and not a given, somebody else will have to tell
me. The challenge to find what I am by becoming other than I am
can only come from someone other than me, by some person addressing me who is new and strange to me and communicates that
strangeness. *My* humanity is *our* mutual work. This second axiom
is a slightly less platitudinous set of anthropological propositions,
and its consequences have—despite Buberizing on all hands—
hardly been looked at at all.

Being man, therefore, is an enterprise rather than a condition. It is, moreover, an inescapably joint enterprise. I am man
only in that I become it; and this enterprise requires more than
one in the same way as marrying or playing football requires
more than one.

Moreover, the enterprise of being human is also a *fearsome*
enterprise—again like marrying or playing football. For who, after all, is to speak this word which can call me to my true self?
You are—and that is what is fearsome. I am dependent on you.
I am dependent on your sensitivity to perceive when I need
your word; on your judgment to find the right one; on your com-
passion to risk speaking it. That is, I am dependent for my
humanity on yours. And that is a risky bet.

There is not only risk here, there is mystery. For if I am dependent upon your humanity for mine, on whom are you dependent for yours? On me. No matter how many members we bring
into this circle, it remains a circle. How does it ever begin to
turn? The common enterprise of man, within which each of
us is man, is the enterprise of mutual availability or—let us
use the word—of love. This common enterprise seems to hang
in time by its own bootstraps. It is obviously impossible that it
should ever have begun, and yet it happens.

It is, I suggest, at the point of this mystery that we speak of
"God"—who is therefore a hiding and a hidden God, for he is

the mystery of our existence. He is the mystery that we do some-how live as response to a word that has not yet been spoken.

The fearsomeness of the human enterprise is not merely the fearsomeness of relatively high risk; it is the fearsomeness of mystery. We are called to live for a future which is not merely not in our own hands but is in unknown hands. We must live by each other, knowing not merely that we are mutually relatively untrustworthy, but with the endlessly reciprocal wait-ing of each for the other to speak, which keeps even our relative trustworthiness from getting started.

Our lives, we have said, are response to an address we have not yet heard, and this is what is meant by the hiddenness of God. The situation is one to which we do not stand up. There is no saying we might not have stood up to it; but we do not. The way we break is that we deal with the futurity and hiddenness of our humanity by defending ourselves against them, and that we use our communication with each other, the mutuality of our existence, to close ourselves to each other.

We wait endlessly for the word of love: each of us from the other, for none of us dares speak it first. If I promise myself to you—before you promise yourself to me—I give my life up in that promise. I die. And only your answering promise—of which I cannot be sure—would be my resurrection. And so I wait, and so do you; and the word of love is not spoken, to which our humanity would be the response.

We may ask, of course, which comes first: our collapse before the mystery of our existence, or its fearsomeness. Do we fail be-fore the mystery of our existence because it is so fearsome? Or is it so fearsome because we have failed before it? But to that question we will get no answer, for this is merely a form of the ancient theological conundrum whether God's predestination or man's sin came first. We will get an answer to that question when both God's predestination and our sin have been ful-filled, and not before.

If I now come to speak of Jesus, it is not because he is "the answer" in the sense of ending these dialectics. The dialectics of our enterprise of humanity continue also in faith, only under changed signs. Moreover, the whole preceding analysis has been Christian from the very beginning: a view of man suggested by the Christian message.

But just so I do come to speak of Jesus; for if the recollection which the Church preserves of him is true, then the word of love to which our humanity is the response, and for which we vainly wait, has once been spoken. Jesus of Nazareth interpreted his own existence wholly by his promise to his fellows. Which is to say: He loved and so died. And without *our* response he heard the response of love: In that death he was called to live, though we gave him no answering word of love.

If he lives, then for us also he is not merely an item of the past; then we too may wait to hear from him that word of love. The word by which we might live, to which our humanity is the response, is still yet to be spoken and we do not anticipate it; but we have a guaranteed promise that it will be spoken. The future remains the unknown future; but it is in known hands. And whoever spoke to Jesus that word of love which called him again to life—the word that he awaited from us and did not hear —that is God.

Being man remains an enterprise rather than a condition. But if he is risen, then the enterprise is the *specific* enterprise of finding a role in his self-giving, and it is an enterprise entered on with promise. Being man remains a fearsome enterprise; but if he is risen, then the fearsomeness is that of all true human love It is still true that we must call each other to our humanity, and that we withhold the call from each other; but if he is risen, then he will be one of us and will not wait upon our response. Therefore even when we defend ourselves against our future, it remains ours; and when we reject the word of love, the very rejection certifies the particular word of love he will speak, which is a word to those who reject it.

II

In the rest of this piece I want to examine these dialectics of becoming human both more secularly and more closely. And I propose to do this under two somewhat arbitrarily chosen headings. They are chosen from the Western vocabulary for aspects of humanization; for better or worse the West is where we are. The headings are "reason" and "organization."

A

The concept of reason is fundamentally an *ethical* concept. Rationality or reasonableness is an ideal we hold up before ourselves and struggle to achieve. As with any ethical concept, what is really hidden in the notion of reason is a set of commands. I suggest that these commands are simply the expression, with respect to our knowing, of the two sides of the enterprise of becoming human: its task-character and its mutuality.

The first command is: be prepared to change your mind. To be reasonable is to subject oneself to this command and be trying to fulfill it. Or perhaps the command is better formulated: test your opinions. The ideal of reason is basically a prohibition. I am prohibited from holding my opinions to be true simply because they are my opinions. I am prohibited from holding my opinions to be true simply because I have always entertained them or even because my whole culture has entertained them. Putting the same command slightly differently, the ideal of reason prohibits me from holding my opinions to be true merely because it would be advantageous for me for them to be true. To be reasonable is to be ready to submit all beliefs to whatever is in each case the appropriate test: to the test of experiment and observation, or to the test of argument, or perhaps simply to the test of discussion. The command of reason, therefore, is simply the command to be open to the future in the matter of beliefs. It is the expression of the task-character of human existence, applied now to the cognitive side of human existence.

The policy that I should be ready to submit my opinions to a test seems, of course, to be obvious. Yet the sway of this demand is exceedingly rare in human history. The standard ethos of mankind has rather been to take precisely the fact that an opinion is held as a sanction of its truth. Normally, mankind has submitted its opinions only to the test of antiquity. This is the *mythic* pattern of human existence. Myth equates the deep truth about the world with a description of an originating event before time and of a consequent primal state; and it appropriately finds its own sanction as truth in continuity of opinion back to that beginning. Most of mankind, including many high cultures, is still captive to mythic existence. It is a part of man's breakout from mythic existence and from traditional culture that he breaks through to the willingness to test his beliefs, that he breaks through to acknowledgment of the task-character of his knowledge.

The particular breakout by which we yet live was accomplished in Greece. But Greece's cognitive freedom hardly survived the moment of its birth, except where it was picked up by Christian faith. The great time that we remember when we speak of the supposed gloriously rational and clear-minded Greeks was in fact an extraordinarily short time in the history of Greece; Greek culture itself returned rapidly to mythic dreaming. Christian faith, of course, had the very best reason to pick up this commitment to testing beliefs. For Christian faith awaits a *last judgment*. That is, faith subjects the whole human enterprise, knowledge included, to a test, and to a test which we will never get safely behind us. The adventure and test-character of knowledge is something which Christians have the best possible reasons to affirm and practice.

We are, of course, endlessly ingenious in evading the cognitive adventure. But once we have acknowledged the ethos of rationality, once we have submitted ourselves to the command to test our opinions, we have to cover our evasions by making them look like reason. We have to "rationalize" them. Of those of our opinions which we are unwilling to test, and which we hold because they belong to the substance of our security in the status quo, we are likely to say they are known by some superior variety of rationality. Thus in the Western metaphysical tradition it has been usual to say that some truths about the world are known by direct participation in the mind of God. Conveniently, we let God do the testing of these opinions; we simply take them over and say that as a consequence of being known by direct participation in his mind they are so blindingly clear that to test them on our part would be absurd. If drugs take over God's role in this evasion, little is changed.

The most sophisticated defenses against the command to test are of course those produced by apparent radical obedience to it. There is one such evasion in particular that is very popular just now. Every cognitive attempt, if submitted to the command to test, represents a wager we might lose. I throw my belief on the table, risking whatever part of my life I have committed to that belief. But there is a way of playing on the open-mindedness and endlessness of the adventure by which I excuse myself from putting any money on the wager, by which I excuse myself from letting anything ride on the opinions I submit to the test.

The modern Nietzschean intelligence endlessly sees new sides to every question. Give this intelligence a problem and it can generate new facets of the problem through all eternity. This is a good thing. But the Nietzschean intelligence is liable, like every other, to its particular perversion: the *uncommitted* intelligence, which empties the wager, which evades the possibility of losing anything of myself, by making no bets on any option. So, for example, we reflect that there may be a God, or that there may not be a God, and decide that anyway we will wait and see. In the meantime we try so to live as to come out on top in any event. This appears to be radical openness to the future; but in reality, since the connection of commitment is cut between my life and the future tests to which I submit my beliefs, this ethos is radically reactionary: it allows everything in my life to stay exactly as it was.

The one who has heard of Jesus has heard reason both to submit all beliefs to the test and to bet his life on those beliefs. For he is called to live life as a wager; and he has heard the hope that precisely by losing his life he might find it.

The second command which constitutes the ideal of reason is: submit your beliefs to *public* tests. I am commanded that the tests to which I point in justifying my opinions must be tests which you could also, at least in principle, perform. This command is merely a direct transcription of the other side of man's nature as the gospel sees it: that human existence is a joint enterprise requires that also our knowing be a joint enterprise. That is to say: that I be able to let you in on the reasons for my beliefs, and in such a way that you can judge those reasons.

We come here to the Western empiricist tradition. The point of that tradition is not some arbitrary restriction on what sorts of experience I may have. My experience is what it is, and that is the end of the matter. The point of the empiricist tradition is rather a restriction on how I *use* my experience to back up my claims to knowledge. Private experience is forbidden at this point. Private experience is any aspect or part of experience which, were I to advance it as justification for a knowledge-claim, is such as to prevent my also telling you how to check this use of it by me. The empiricist tradition rejects use of private experiences as clues to truth because truth is a joint enterprise.

The point of the empiricist tradition is not a restriction on what experiences I can have. The point is an analysis of the conditions under which experience can be critically shared. Quite evidently you and I can share experiences only by their mutual reference to our common public world, only by our experience's reference to that world which is neither inside me nor inside you but precisely between us. One may call it the "material" world, or the "sensuous" world, or whatever he likes.

We do not know in advance how many ways there may be of sharing the public world. But any access which I claim to a putative reality, whereby I cannot tell you how to get the same access, is disqualified as an experience relevant to truth. If I say I am experiencing something, you should in general take my word for it; but if I identify my experience by saying I am experiencing "pain" or I am experiencing "God," then to make that identification I use a word out of our joint public language. That a language is public means that you are able to check the statements I make using it: they are statements you too are able to decide to make or not to make.

If humanity is a joint enterprise, then only with this emergence from privacy does our experience become human, does it become knowledge of the truth. My experience in itself is what it is what it is what it is . . . , as an animal's experience is what it is what it is what it is. . . . The privacy and irrefutability of my experience I have as an animal—and there is nothing wrong with that. I *am* an animal, and if I were not, neither would I be anything else. But I am also a man, and I am a man in that I emerge from privacy. I obey the command of humanity when I refrain from claims about human truth which are backed only by my private, that is, prehuman experience. The command to be human enforces, therefore, a sort of asceticism, and much is undoubtedly lost by it. But no one ever said that the creation of man would be without loss.

In itself the demand for reason cannot therefore conflict with the promise of the gospel. Indeed, I suggest it is but an expression of it. Why then do we often speak of faith *versus* reason? Because it can happen that God in fact withdraws from the public realm, or at least that God as a particular culture has understood him withdraws from the public realm of that culture. Then our communication with each other about God, our rational knowledge of him, will indeed become broken and difficult. And then we may be glad that rational human knowledge of God is not all there is to contact with God, that God is our God also as he is God of stones and sticks.

Just here, however, it seems to me that religious people face a terrible temptation, in the attempt to save religion from these difficulties of public communication. We do indeed now experience such difficulties every day: we go into the marketplace and speak of God, and no one knows what we are talking about. Then we face the temptation to save religion by withdrawing it altogether from the demand of reason into the safe realm of private experience. Religion, we will say, is a matter of "intuition" or of "sincerity." We will comfort ourselves that it does not matter what one believes, i.e., it does not matter what his public expression is, just so he is sincere inwardly about it. It is important to understand clearly that by this retreat we do not overcome the difficulties which the demand for reason does indeed, in the circumstance of God's silence, make for religion. By these means we simply capitulate altogether.

Believers in Christ, in any case, should not need this escape.

Perhaps religion can be saved by this retreat, but not Christian faith. If we have heard the gospel, then we have heard reason to persist in seeking our God in the public arena. For then we have heard of a revelation under a man named Pontius Pilate, and of a God who will verify himself by judging the quick and the dead, i.e., the entire public history of man. We are therefore called to say our piece about God in the open arena of all nations or not say it at all. And we are promised that the gates of hell will not at last prevail against this attempt. The effort of faith will always be to hold our ultimate concerns in the human realm of communication, and to fight all weariness which would drop them back to the level of private prehuman experience. And this effort is one which has promise.

B

Organization has two roots. (1) The mutuality of human existence means that each of us is himself only as part of a larger whole he makes with others—only as an organ of a community. That I am an organ of a community is not a limitation of my humanity, it is its possibility. (2) If this community is to be open to the future, if it is not to dissolve under the impact of every change that comes along, then some of these organs must be continuing organs, and not merely ad hoc arrangements for particular occasions. That is to say, the community must be organized. The need of organization is therefore rooted in the mutuality and futurity of man. It is one of the requisites of human existence, and perfecting our organization is one of the ways we become human.

But we all know too well how we regularly turn this organization against our chances for humanity. It is exactly our organization which gives us opportunities to receive the shock of the future creatively, but instead of taking those opportunities, we spend our time tending the organization itself, so as to wall ourselves up behind it in the status quo. That we may be anti-establishment types does not guarantee us against this at all—

currently the Movement spends more time on its own non-organization than on anything else.

Perhaps here is the main problem which now disturbs us about American life: the way in which status quo answers are built into the very structure of the decision-making machinery. On every issue, the organs of our society go through an elaborate dance, approach the very verge of change, and then produce the answer one knew all along would emerge: keep on with things as they are. Thus there have been years of agitation in the matter of the Vietnamese War, agitation which brought down a president—and the end result of it was that we recently heard Mr. Nixon give the same speech, in some places nearly verbatim, that Mr. Johnson used to give regularly.

Organization is nothing but the structure of our mutuality, and yet it turns incorrigibly against that mutuality. As has been repeatedly pointed out, the more highly organized a society, the more does our relation to each other occur through secondary roles: in such roles, it is not Robert Jenson but Professor so-and-so that needs your attention, it isn't John Jacobowski but the bus conductor who confronts your morning. Harvey Cox is undoubtedly right in saying that the dominance of secondary roles in megalopolis is an opportunity of greater freedom, but this is true only for a very few. New York City is indeed for people like us an opportunity of greater freedom than Gettysburg provides. But most people who live in New York City experience the dominance of secondary roles in their human contacts as alienating and dehumanizing. The very organization by which we live with each other prevents us from getting at each other.

Technology exacerbates this character of organization. We will consider just one example: data processing. A "bureau" is merely a primitive data-processing mechanism, so that the replacement of a bureau by a computer is only a modest technological advance. But the consequences are great. Computers operate with binary arithmetic. So far as arithmetic is concerned, this creates no problems. But when we store such things as census responses or credit ratings in memory banks, the binary logic of computers dictates that the simplest way to do it is in the form of yes-or-no questions and responses. Out of the stored information, new questions will then be generated to ask us—and the difficulty is that the options posed will emerge from previous yes-or-no answers. Just thereby, the range of our future is narrowed.

We can, of course, fight this. Questions can be put with three options, or ten or twenty, and then translated from arithmetics on these bases into binary arithmetic for storage. But there is a point at which we will tire of this; and in fact programmers do not do much of it and cannot be expected to. The narrowing of our human options as a result of frail humans using computers is already a very real phenomenon—as any of you will know who have tried to get a mistake rectified in a computerized business office.

It should be no surprise, therefore, that history is dotted with rebellions against organization, or that we have such a deep rebellion against it now. But how would we go about being *un*organized? One tack now much in vogue is to make all mutuality momentary, so that it shall need little organization. We do not marry; we have meetings which are "beautiful" precisely because they do not impose on the future bondage to past commitments. But by this means what we do is transform life into a mere series of status quos, and in fact abandon freedom altogether. Another tack is to radically simplify communities, to the point where they need very little organization. Monks have tried to do this all through history; and communes try to do it now. A dozen or so communes scattered around Gettysburg would undoubtedly be a very good thing—as salt; but they are no solution to the problem, for to the extent to which this endeavor of simplifying society succeeds, we return to tribal society—which is the most static and rigidly structured of all.

As I have argued elsewhere[1] the problem is the problem of the center, of what holds us together to be a community. If it is only the organization itself, or some ideology, that holds the community together, then that organization will indeed try to enslave us. For only personal address, only your real personal challenge to

---

[1] See Chapter 5, "Eschatological Politics and Political Eschatology."

me and mine to you, can set free. Societies have therefore regularly sought to put persons at their centers—royal families, divinized heroes, dictators, or what you will. But these attempts too have regularly proved destructive. For only that king or hero whose word to me was a word of love could center our society as a society of freedom; and where are we to find such a person? Unless, of course, Jesus of Nazareth should really be as we have remembered him, and really be alive and coming to us. In that case, we may indeed await a society with a personal center, a society bound together by one who speaks to all other members of the society the word of love.

Meanwhile, what we have to do is anticipate the end-society, but anticipate it not gnostically but historically. I suggest this means a sort of unresolvable union of anarchism with devotion to the organization. We are at once cheerfully to refuse to be repressed by the organization, and devoted to the society so organized and even to the improvement of its organization. As protest marchers, we should carry the black flag in one hand and the Stars and Stripes in the other. We should build bigger and better data-processors, and occasionally slip them a folded card.

III

Perhaps I can sum up all I have been trying to say about becoming man under one final heading, also taken from the vocabulary of Western humanism: "creativity."

Creativity is not a particular faculty of man, so as perhaps to conflict with other faculties, as reason or will. Man's creativity is rather his entire thrust through time, accomplished as rationality and as organization and as an indefinite number of other aspects. Man looks back at himself as he lies back there, as he is already a product, and picks this past reality up and uses it as the block of stone out of which he carves himself anew.

We may dare this adventure, and every day invent ourselves afresh, because we are not the only creators. What *we* do with our creativity is merely to pile up raw material for love (in love, openness to the future and mutuality definitively meet). The story I will at my end have written will be delivered over to Christ and to you, as a unique and particular set of possibilities for your love—and vice versa. We can, that is, dare the adventure of creativity because there is one who will not wait for the rest of us to be absolutely free and absolutely mutual—to be human.

7

Mission as Revolution

Carl E. Braaten

Because of my own background in the overseas missions of the Church, I have become increasingly more concerned to develop a theology of mission within the horizon of the revolutionary ferment of the "third world." What is the biblical basis for such a theology? Although I have previously written a number of times on the hermeneutical problem, here for the first time I advance the idea of a revolutionary hermeneutic of the Bible. Such a hermeneutic helps us to read the Bible as the history of liberation, from the exodus to the kingdom of God.

I

THE POLITICIZING OF ESCHATOLOGY

The world mission programs of Western Churches are in serious trouble. Some people believe that we are reaching the end of the missionary era. It is quite easy to see what is wrong on the surface. In fact, hardly anything seems right. They are white, Western and rich; they are stained by the isms of their colonial origins—imperialism, racism, militarism, capitalism, sectarianism, and proselytism. The white missionary did not, of course, see it this way. His own self-understanding was innocent to the point of being naively a-political. He was after all only bringing the message of eternal salvation to souls who were otherwise damned to hell. Mission work was carried out under the rubric of personal evangelism. I think this focus of mission has become fuzzy. The missionary who is sent overseas today is rarely involved in personal evangelism, but the theology of mission he learned probably did not prepare him for a clear alternative. Missionaries today are not really sure of what they are supposed to be doing. And so many of them resign after one term.

My title already suggests that there is an alternative to personal evangelism. Mission is the politicizing of eschatology.[1] It cannot stay at ease within the privatizing tendencies of personal evangelism. A political grounding of eschatology is needed today, first of all, as a corrective to the tendency to let the gospel fall into the sphere of personal and private concerns, thus ignoring the social and political conditions of human existence, and secondly as a corrective to a transcendental eschatology that docetically leaps beyond the incarnational plane of history into the beyond or the hereafter.

The correction we are speaking of is not merely a clever tactic to make the gospel relevant today. The corrective impulses must arise from the gospel itself. That gospel is the good news of the kingdom of God. This symbol of the kingdom of God cannot be shorn of its political aspect by reducing it to the personalistic sphere of the I-Thou relationship. The Lutheran tradition shows a marked tendency to do this. This is particularly noticeable in Einar Billing's wonderful little book, *Our Calling*. There he sets forth the amazing rule: "Never believe that you have a correct understanding of a thought of Luther before you have succeeded in reducing it to a simple corollary of the thought of the forgiveness of sins."[2] Billing would have us "understand clearly that the forgiveness of sins means ultimately nothing less than the totality of all the ways God has taken in history to build his kingdom. The kingdom of God is nothing else than the actualization of the forgiveness of sins."[3] This is realized eschatology with a vengeance. The inwardly personal sphere has swallowed up the political and social characteristics of the kingdom

---

[1] See how this idea is spelled out in Johannes B. Metz's essay, "The Church and the World in the Light of a 'Political Theology'," *Theology of the World*, trans. by William Glen-Doepel (Herder and Herder, 1969), pp. 107-124.

[2] Einar Billing, *Our Calling*, trans. by Conrad Bergendoff (Fortress Press, 1947), p. 4.

[3] *Ibid.*, p. 16.

of God.[4] The attempt to summarize the gospel under this heading of "forgiveness of sins" is largely responsible for setting in motion what Johannes B. Metz has called the "trend toward the private."[5] On the other hand, the return to the full concept of the kingdom of God can help us to sound the political and social notes of the Christian message, and thus avoid cutting everything in Christianity down to the size of the personal or interpersonal. It would be better to see forgiveness as the existentially most acute way that the power of God's fulfilling future impresses itself upon the individual in the present. The political and social relevance of the kingdom of God is not thereby exhausted in the event of personal forgiveness. Eschatology strives for ever more adequate actualization in the open fields of public life, so that the eschatological realities of freedom, peace, and justice may achieve provisional embodiment in institutional structures that determine the conditions under which individuals exist in society. Eschatology that is not grounded politically becomes a quietive, an opiate, an ideological servant of the status quo.

If we grant that the eschatological promises of the kingdom are working in history to become reality, that the present task of mission is the politicizing of eschatology, then we cannot escape the possibility that the specific terms of such politicizing may spell revolution. Now what do we mean by revolution? The word has become rubbery; it can be stretched to mean a lot of different things. This does not, however, make it more useless than many other great words. Some precision can be introduced. In its narrowest sense it can mean simply the overthrowing of an established political order. It should be obvious that this sort of intervention in politics is not the proper business of the Christian mission. But in a wider sense revolution means a fundamental change that is brought about in the social as well as the political structures. Revolution does not mean changing things *in* the system; that is merely reform. It means, rather, a chang-

---

[4] For a systematic theological description of the characteristics of the kingdom of God, see Paul Tillich, *Systematic Theology* (Universitiy of Chicago Press, 1963), pp. 358ff.

[5] Johannes B. Metz, *Theology of the World*, p. 109.

ing *of* the system in its very core. This is the sense of revolution which the missionary movement must accept into its theory and practice if it is to be reactivated by its eschatological beginnings and achieve a new relevancy in the present world situation.

II

A REVOLUTIONARY HERMENEUTIC OF THE BIBLE

Is a realignment of mission with revolution possible on biblical grounds? I believe it is, but a theology of revolution requires a revolutionary hermeneutic of the Bible.[6] The Bible is a revolutionary document because it is a book of radical promises which have yet to be fulfilled. Christ sums up all these promises in himself, and he is God's word of guarantee that they shall all be fulfilled. "He is the Yes pronounced upon God's promises, every one of them."[7] But before they shall all be fulfilled, a lot of changes will have to be made in the foundations of existing reality. In the biblical picture of reality a revolutionary break with the old order of things is required by the approaching new reality of the future. The entire thrust of the prophets and the apostles was toward a wonderfully new reality that was coming into its own. Mission is the agency of this new reality and world history is the field in which the divine experiment is going on whether something new can come from something old, whether new life can be born from the graveyards of humanity. The Bible ends just when the mission had barely begun. In the meantime, the world has not become completely transformed. A terrific disparity continues between what we experience in the world and what God promises with his kingdom, between what we see and what we hope. We hope for something positively new and a fulfilling future for all men. But what we see is oppression and hunger; we see misery and emptiness; we see slavery and humiliation. In the Bible we see mankind expelled

[6] Cf. Jürgen Moltmann, "Toward a Political Hermeneutic of the Gospel," *Religion, Revolution and the Future,* trans. by M. Douglas Meeks (Charles Scribner's Sons, 1969), pp. 93ff.

[7] 1 Cor. 1:20 (N. E. B.).

from a garden; we see a people groaning under its burdens in slavery; we see a people in exile in a foreign land; we see a people chafing under alien rule; we see the representative body of all mankind nailed to a cross. What makes the Bible revolutionary is its persistent announcement that ultimate reality is the power to change all that. It proclaims God as the future of all mankind in which all the negations of the present will be negated; even the death of death itself will happen. A consciousness that is stimulated by the biblical vision of new things will be restless with anger amid the deprivations of the present.

The Bible must be read as subversive literature, since it locates the meaning of history in the struggle of God for the liberation of the oppressed. Any book that makes people love freedom and propels them to the front lines of the liberation movement in history must understandably be placed on the index of books prohibited by the ruling establishment. The fact that the Bible happens, however, to be a best seller in today's society must mean that it is being misread as one of the harmless classics of world literature, as just part of the healthy diet of more or less nice religious people. Its revolutionary claims are then robbed of their force, either by being wholly deferred to another world or by demythologizing them to conform to the actual present. A revolutionary hermeneutic will reopen the Bible as a dangerous book and extremely one-sided, since it shows God taking sides against those enthroned with pride and privilege, with power and riches. ". . . he has scattered the proud in the imagination of their hearts, he has put down the mighty from their thrones, and exalted those of low degree; he has filled the hungry with good things, and the rich he has sent empty away."[8] This thought might provoke the missionary movement to engage in partisan warfare, to take sides with the poor and oppressed in every land, and to lead the way in the struggle for new and higher forms of freedom.[9]

---

[8] Luke 1:51-53 (R. S. V.).

[9] See Jürgen Moltmann, "God in Revolution," *Religion, Revolution and the Future* (Charles Scribner's Sons, 1969), p. 140. He writes, "In the present struggles for freedom and justice, Christians must side with the humanity of the oppressed."

III
THE POWER OF NEGATIVE THINKING

The recasting of mission in a revolutionary role cannot be carried out on biblical grounds alone. A revolutionary hermeneutic is highly tendentious, but so is every other one. Each hermeneutical approach is bound up with one's view of man and the world. But our choice of hermeneutic is not purely arbitrary. If we view man and his world in terms of history driving toward the future, we owe it in large part to the eschatological perspective in the Bible. In fact, our concept of revolution as implying the possibility of fundamental change toward something really new presupposes the categories of history and eschatology.[10]

The Futuricity of Man

Revolution is an historical possibility grounded in man's unique capacity to bring the realm of the future to the fore of his consciousness. Man's mind is not merely a receptacle for the knowledge of facts about what is dead and gone or actually here and now; it is more importantly a receiving set picking up signals about new possibilities. These possibilities may crystallize into a challenging and inspiring vision of the future. That is the way it happened in the Bible. The image of the kingdom of God became a powerful symbol of hope, representing both personal and social fulfillment. It is a kingdom in which bodily and spiritual ills are healed, in which peace reigns among all creatures, and in which love and justice finally work in harmony for the good of all. Where this image becomes the driving power of our life, it will generate convictions that seem to me to be potentially revolutionary.

Where life is leaning forward in hope toward the coming of God's kingdom, it means that we break the back of the present, whether that present seems like a vale of tears, driving us to despair, or like the best of all possible worlds, making us satisfied

---

[10] See Wolfhart Pannenberg, "Facts of History and Christian Ethics," *Dialog* (Autumn, 1969), where he offers an outline for an ethics of social change on the basis of a theology of history.

with things as they are. To decide for the kingdom of God means that life as we now know it isn't all there's to it. Life will not always be like this and so things do not have to be like this. We want to see things changed. We are overwhelmed by a "great refusal" (H. Marcuse) to let the laws of the present ruin our hopes for the future. We have a call from the future to add new dimensions according to the vision that inspires us.

To have an eschatology implies that the essence of things lies in their future, that therefore everything that exists is still alienated from what it essentially will be. It is revolutionary to think that whatever exists has to be radically changed in order to become what it really is. There is nothing so whole and holy that we have a right to say: Hands off! Nothing so fixed and established that it cannot, must not, be changed. The kingdom of God approaches with the call for a radical conversion of what we are and have; it comes not with the judgment of the law that has been accumulated through the past, but with the law of judgment that falls from the eschatological future, over which none of us has any control. I take it this means that we cannot afford to be traditionalists, as scribes who merely know their legal precedents.

To have an eschatology is to claim to know something about the world as it ought to be. We live in a society that has the means, but has lost track of the ends; so the means become the ends.

In Christianity eschatology is the constant; the ethics are variable. The Christian mission must keep hitting home on the question of ends, however much its language about a coming new reality might sound idealistic or utopian. It is just this relentless pressing of a transcendent image of the new future upon the present structures that can recharge the mission with revolutionary power. The present order is confronted by a dimension beyond itself about which a claim to greater validity is being made. That has the effect of relativizing the present; in fact it can so anachronize it that we can say with Paul that what is present is not really the new we are looking for, but is just the hanging on of the old. Paul had a criterion for it: new is what corresponds to the eschatological reality that has appeared in Christ. Anything else is old, even if it is the latest thing.

So there can be new things in the past, and old things in the future, depending on their relation to the qualitative future that happened in the person of Jesus.

A Critical View of Society

The picture of the future that takes shape in the imagination of faith can drive us into radical opposition to the system of things as they are. We can reach the point where we feel that society must turn itself about, that things can't go on as they are, that the present trends and structures are demonic and have forfeited their right to claim our support. We have a loyalty to the future that implies a clear-cut caesura with the established state of affairs. We become schizophrenics of the kingdom, because meanwhile we go on living in the world as integral parts of the system of oppression that we are driven to criticize. No one has expressed more eloquently this split within the revolutionary Christian consciousness than St. Paul. He confessed that he was in the agonizing situation of doing things he hated, that the instinctual structure of his life pulled him in the opposite direction from the loyalty of his mind.[11] Revolutionaries who are filled with eschatological madness are easy prey to self-righteousness and moral perfectionism. The faults they find in others or in "the system" they often fail to trace in themselves.[12] They need the sobering self-awareness of Paul in Romans 7. Yet, they should not turn this around and say that since they are no better than others, they have no right to criticize. The truth of the message does not ride on the purity of the preacher. The schizophrenic situation must be endured.

Our service to the present may take the form of fanning the flames of the future that burn critically within it. The eschatolo-

[11] Romans 7:15-23.

[12] In the epilogue to his book, *A Theology for Radical Politics*, Michael Novak winces at the purity of the young militants. "Moreover, there is moral pretension and class snobbery in the purity which many of the young try to maintain in themselves . . . It is a mistake to think of them as the bearers of God's truth of moral wisdom, the darlings of nature, history, or manifest destiny. Those who supported Prohibition also thought of themselves as especially pure. Self-righteousness is a deeply rooted American form" (Herder and Herder, 1969), p. 124.

gical outlook is the motor power of criticism, of negative think-ing toward the present. Herbert Marcuse has recently written in defense of a faculty he feels is nearly lost in our society, namely, the power of negative thinking.[13] To me that sounds more Christian in a world of sin and death than Norman Vin-cent Peale's "power of positive thinking." Thinking that is nur-tured by eschatology can be expressed in Hegel's words as "es-sentially the negation of that which is immediately before us."[14] The reason this faculty is weak is that Christianity does not preach, let alone practice, its own eschatology, and no other promising image of the future has arisen in today's culture to take its place. Instead, many of the prophets in modern times have countered eschatology with the bad news about our hopeless present. They have busied themselves with what Frederick Polak calls the "iconoclasm of the images of the future"[15] and thus help to fulfill their prophecies about the vacuum in reality that lies ahead. This futureless outlook may evoke a cry of heroic de-spair in the existentialist, but it only succeeds in handing the world over to the powers that prevail at present, as though that were good enough, or if not, nothing can be done anyway to change it. This is exactly what the ideologues of the status quo want people to do with their feelings of alienation—turn them in upon themselves so that they do not focus outwardly on creative al-ternatives to the established forms of life. The positivist who realistically sticks with the given facts and measurable operations has the field to himself. For him there is a presumption in favor of that which is, just because it is. He is king in the one-dimen-sional society that Herbert Marcuse writes about in all his recent books. This is a society which stands without opposition; there is no antithesis, no power of negative thinking, no agency which is not effectively absorbed into society as one of its smooth running parts. The major institutions of society—big govern-ment, big business, big labor, big military, big university—are all joined in a conspiracy to keep the present system going at

[13] Herbert Marcuse, *Reason and Revolution* (Beacon Press, 1960), p. vii.
[14] *Ibid.*
[15] Frederick L. Polak, *The Image of the Future,* trans. by Elise Boulding (Ocean Publications, 1961), Vol. II, pp. 29 and 66ff.

all costs. Technology is used as a tool to make the system totalitarian, a total system of domination. That is not merely an internal condition of our advanced industrial society. The system extends its reach around the world, using every means of penetration—economic, political, cultural, and even direct military intervention. The gap between the affluence of the rich and the poverty of the poor widens every year. The approach of the system to internal problems is welfare; its approach to external problems is warfare. And most of us are so pacified by the ideology of this system that we are afraid even to consider any real alternatives. It is at this point of our helpless conformity to the way things are that the mission might be recharged by its revolutionary hope for humanity to mount a counter-offensive against the irrational system. For if the Church is true to her calling to be at the front line of the kingdom's ingression into this world, she can never be just one of the smooth-running parts of the social system. The Church above all has the task to regenerate the power of negative thinking in the world because she bears a transcending message that "overshoots"[16] every model of individual and social life that mankind has yet succeeded in realizing. This is the basis for mission as permanent revolution in history.

IV

MISSION AS MILITANT ESCHATOLOGY

Finally, I would like to advance some symbols by which mission might be seen in a more revolutionary light. They may help to encapsulate what I am trying to say.

[16] I have taken this concept from Marcuse. He writes, "The terms 'transcend' and 'transcendence' are used througout in the empirical, critical sense: they designate tendencies in theory and practice which, in a given society, 'overshoot' the established universe of discourse and action toward its historical alternatives (real possibilities)." It is an indictment on the Church that Marcuse did not have in mind Christian eschatology as the source of a transcendent criticism of society, releasing tendencies that "overshoot" what has become established in society: Herbert Marcuse, *One Dimensional Man* (London: Routledge & Kegan Paul Ltd., 1964), p. xi, n. 1.

Mission is militant eschatology. Its military target is all that is negative in the present. It is the negation of the negative. To appropriate an apt expression from Marcuse, "The language of negation [is] the Great Refusal to accept the rules of a game in which the dice are loaded."[17] Mission is a subversive movement. It looks at that which is in the light of what it lacks. It holds that you more quickly come to the truth about a society when you look not at what it includes, but at what it excludes. If a society is a wonderful place of opportunity for me, but a hell for my brother, it is a wretched place for both of us. It is the task of mission to identify the source of this wretchedness and to lay bare the real contradictions in society, to make way for qualitative change.

Mission is partisanship with the poor. It is solidarity with the outcasts and outsiders, the exploited and alienated. It is alliance with the ghetto population in capitalist countries, with the blacks in racist societies, with young intellectuals and artists whose voice for freedom is stifled by military dictatorships, with students who see no real option to a system of education that services the establishment they find so repulsive, and with the "external proletariat" in the Third World.[18]

Mission is the laboratory of freedom. A transcendent vision of freedom must become a driving political force to explode all repressive and authoritarian forms of control. The Church is in fact to be a microcosm of the possibilities of a free world. The man who joins the Church should be able to sense that he is entering the home of the free. Faith always opens up new fronts in its fight for freedom, according to the form of slavery that prevails. We do not know what freedom is positively, for freedom is the essence of God. But the history of faith gives us negative knowledge of freedom: freedom from the idolatry of nature in the Old Testament, freedom from the works of the law in Paul's Letters, freedom from the cult of the state in John's *Revelation,* freedom from a Christian emperor in the Investiture Controversy, freedom from an infallible papacy in the Reformation, freedom from heteronomous authority in the Enlighten-

---

[17] Herbert Marcuse, *Reason and Revolution,* p. x.
[18] Herbert Marcuse, *An Essay on Liberation* (Beacon Press, 1969), p. 80.

ment, freedom from economic servitude in modern socialism, although by this time faith's fight for freedom often had to be carried on under secular auspices against the enslaving institutions and dogmas of Christendom.[19] The fight for freedom must go on. The forms of slavery are as gripping today as ever, only in a secular society they appear more in terms of history and politics than in terms of the more familiar biblical pattern of nature and religion. The Christian mission is often so irrelevant because it carries faith's fight for freedom onto fronts that have long since been abandoned by the kingdom of God.

Mission is modeling a new style of life. It seeks to fashion a new sensorium, a percipient center, which is open to the impulses and insights of love that flash in upon us from the Spirit of God. No law and no order can contain the qualitative change that the future of God lays upon us. As a sacrament of the new world that is promised to humanity, the Church can now celebrate life, its good things and happy times. Christians do not have to be up-tight like other battle-weary warriors. They can bring joy into the valleys of the sorrowing and disillusioned. They can be light, happy, loose, and buoyed by humor, because the currency with which they negotiate the business of life is backed by something more precious than silver or gold. But this love is not merely for personal comfort and enjoyment. It is a seed with which the Church is to impregnate society, so that the unborn future of the world may be formed at all levels of life, including its social and political structures.

If the kingdom of God has social and political character, as we have maintained, then the Church must accept a corresponding responsibility in mission. And this responsibility has revolutionary implications, because the eschatological ground of mission reveals the negative conditions under which this world exists.

[19] For a brief summary of the story of freedom, see Jürgen Moltmann's essay, "The Revolution of Freedom: Christians and Marxists Struggle for Freedom," *Religion, Revolution and the Future, op. cit.,* pp. 63ff.

8

A Theology for
Student Activism

Carl E. Braaten

Like others who teach in theological schools, I have experienced a
challenge from the new breed of seminarians who bring a radical political consciousness with them to theology. I have tried to
show that theology is not necessarily the prerogative of conservatives "who have their heads screwed on backward," although
theological professors appear as such to not a few students who
have had a taste of student politics in their college days. This
originated as an address to a group of seminarians involved in a
week of orientation at the Catholic Theological Union in Chicago,
and bears all the marks of the spoken word.

My title, "A Theology for Student Activism," is clearly worded
on the model of Michael Novak's book, *A Theology for Radical
Politics.* But that is as far as I can go in promising any similarity,
for whereas he does talk about student politics and radical
change, the theological base from which he operates is one
which entails discarding what he disparagingly calls "Germanic
eschatology" in favor of "Mediterranean nature."[1] In a footnote
he cites Jürgen Moltmann's *Theology of Hope* as the latest example of this Germanic eschatology whose restless drive toward the
future he feels to be "dangerous." But I like what Novak set out
to do, namely, "to bring a radical Christian theology to the support of the student movement of the present generation."[2]

In setting forth a *theology* for student activism it is not my
intention to deal with student activism as such. You can read
about that in the daily papers. And I don't even intend to deal

[1] Michael Novak, *A Theology for Radical Politics* (Herder & Herder,
1969), p. 110.
[2] *Ibid.,* p. 17.

133

with the activism of theological students. That could be better described by a student who has been active in various organizations and who can report what each one is up to and which one is now out-radicalizing all the others. Rather, I want to reflect on student activism from a theological perspective, and perhaps invite it to seek that radicalism that gets down to the roots of the Christian faith.

I
STUDENT ACTIVISM AS THE FERMENT OF HOPE

In his *Essay on Liberation,* Herbert Marcuse characterizes the student movement today as "the ferment of hope."[3] I want to second that, for hope is the soul of student activism today. It can be called the ferment of hope because it seeks to open up the world to its unfinished future. It presupposes that history has not come to an end, that really new things are still in store for us. It tries to interrupt the monologue of this "one-dimensional society" to force it into a dialogue with the future. When the radical students at the University of Chicago occupied the administration building last year, one of their spokesmen was able to boil down into one phrase their many criticisms of the education they were getting: they never study the future. Theirs is basically a positivistic education which accepts the world as it is and bows down before it in a mood of analytic humility.

I welcome student activism as a fight against the ideology of the establishment, whose refrain is "there's nothing you can do to change things." This refrain can be heard in a number of versions. There's nothing you can do to change things, because things are what natural law and the sacred traditions of the past have made them. There is a fixity about them, and you are fools to knock your heads against the granite structures of the well-established order. There's nothing you can do to change things; the most you can hope is to improve things by playing ball according to the rules that men with experience and PhD's happen to have decided are best for you. There's nothing you can do to

[3] Herbert Marcuse, *An Essay on Liberation* (Beacon Press, 1969), p. 60.

change things; your feelings of frustration, however, are perfectly understandable. Why, when we were students we were like that too. It's just part of the pains of growing up. There's nothing in the student movement that the "oedipal theory" can't explain. There's nothing you can do to change things, because although things are admittedly not perfect, they're no worse now than they've ever been. And they'll never be any different in the future. Who was the wise old Frenchman who said, "The more things change, the more they remain the same"? It is easy to unmask these realisms as nothing but cop-outs for people who have become cozy in the world as it is.

Student activism is a movement in search of creative alternatives to the forms of life students have experienced and to the way they see the system working. The corner of the world they know best is, of course, the educational system. They have gone to school all their lives. In Greek the linguistic root of school is *scholé* meaning "free time." But the schooling students have experienced is not free, but laden with heavy pressures and alienating drudgery. School is a concentration camp of students grubbing for grades and competing with one another for a bigger prize in the real world after graduation. When students finish college and enter a theological seminary, they come with greater expectations. They hope that seminary will not be a mere extension of college. But what they find is often what they had hoped to leave behind. Having been overcharged with hope, they are now overburdened with disappointment. They find that their classmates are still competitors, not confreres. They are still in a diploma factory, not in a spiritual community. They are still raw material for a product the system has pre-designed. They balk at the prospects of becoming spare parts for the ecclesiastical machinery that to them seems worn out. They protest against a curriculum they fear will standardize them so that they become more relevant to the desires of the Church and her existing structures than to the impulses of the gospel and real human need. The result is student revolt. This is the new thing in theological education, namely, the trend toward the politicizing of the student consciousness.

Now, one could say that student politics in a theological seminary is not new. We had it in our day. But what we had was different. Politically-minded students would run for office, win, and then play the game with the loaded dice of the school administration. We envied these guys who could talk things over with the president and deans and carry out their instructions. But today student activism implies radical distrust of such conventional institutionalized roles. Student government has collapsed at our school; you can't give away the job of student body president. Nobody wants to be appointed or elected to anything. To some this looks like "bugging out," as adolescent unwillingness to accept responsibility. I think the opposite is at least partly true, for the lack of desire to accept institutionalized roles may be linked with a strong addiction to try new things, and therefore to improvise outside the regular channels. Student activism is so transient and fluid because it turns upon issues, rather than lodging itself in offices that ride on the back of an established institution. It is just this addiction to try new things beyond institutional roles that leads us to speak of the student movement as a "ferment of hope."

But why, we might ask, are student activists in theological schools much less extremist than in the better universities? If the crisis in our nation is the cause of youth militancy in general, why isn't the crisis in the Church causing an equally intense radicalism among young Christians? That is very disturbing to me. Instead, what we see among young people is that when they are really turned off by the way things are, and feel driven to a radical stance, they do not go looking for it within the circle of Christian options, but settle for some point along the spectrum of Trotskyism, Maoism, Leninism, Castroism, or some antithetical ism on the far right. There are two possible explanations to this, one sociological, the other theological, and I think the answer is a mixture of both.

The sociological consideration is that the radicals among university students are, on the whole, not anticipating a future for themselves in national politics.[4] They can afford to be extremist

⁴ Ian Weinberg and Kenneth N. Walker, "Student Politics and Political Systems: Toward a Typology," *American Journal of Sociology* (July, 1969), Vol. 75, No. 1, pp. 77-94.

because they never expect to have to run for public office. They are part of a student political sub-culture that enjoys a high degree of freedom. Richard Flacks has shown that a majority of activists tend to be the brightest students, coming from above average socio-economic backgrounds.[5] Most of these define for themselves a future outside the political system by rejecting careers in law and business and medicine and the mass media. They are oriented to the university and will probably find their future within it. This is not the case with theological students. There are built-in links between the seminary and the Church. Their future vocation in the Church places constraints on their activities in the seminary. The seminary is not as insulated from the Church, structurally speaking, as the university is from the political system. A student who fails or is blacklisted in the seminary has no future in the Church under which that seminary functions.

The theological consideration is that the gospel has ceased to be a radical message in the Churches which exist to proclaim it. The only alternative to a conservative traditionalism that has its head screwed on backward is a liberalism which is a watered down religion of middle-class convenience. The potential source of a Christian radicalism is the eschatological message of Jesus which inflamed the earliest apostolic mission. Now eschatology is a current fad in theology, and we are hard put to define it in an unambiguous way. It is almost impossible to mention even the word without getting impaled on a theological dispute or without going mad with all its variant meanings. But three things we can say: first, eschatology was central in Jesus' own thinking; he preached the kingdom of God as the oncoming power of the future that determines the destiny of all things; second, he so opened himself to the power of God's future in radical obedience that the powers-that-be racked him up on a cross to die; third, whenever that eschatology and that cross—the *eschatologia crucis*—became the driving passion of Christians, they were able to bear the torch of hope in society that lightens the way that men may go. Eschatology has let loose streams of anticipation that keep the pres-

---

[5] Richard Flacks, "The Liberated Generation: An Exploration of the Roots of Student Protest," *Journal of Social Issues* (July, 1969), 23, pp. 52-75.

ent alive to possibilities that Jesus pioneered for the world through his living and dying and rising. Student activism is, indeed, charged with hope, but what it needs is to get plugged into the socket of a Christian radicalism whose juices flow from the powerhouse of biblical eschatology. If student activists would protest that they can do completely without any Christian partnership or biblical sponsorship, I would have to reply, "Maybe! I doubt it! But in any case, the Church and her theology have much to gain from the initiatives of student activism." Let us spell this out.

II
VIEWING THINGS FROM THE BOTTOM UP

In an essay entitled, "The American Revolution Seen from the Bottom Up," Jesse Lemisch has advanced the thesis that you can more accurately get at the truth about a society if you view it from the bottom up, if you share the viewpoint of the powerless and the inarticulate. His assumption is that history is recorded by those who rule in society, and they are precisely the ones who have the most to hide.[6] Similarly, the student movement through its sympathy with the poor and the blacks is causing us to look at our society from the bottom up, or from the outside in. That is a challenge to the Church and her theology, which we ought to recognize as a leaf out of our own past.

The Bible is a book written from the bottom up. Israel has told us what it was like to be on the outside, an outcast pariah-people, chosen by historical Destiny to suffer and to wander, to be a half-starved child of the desert, to be a slave people overburdened by work, to be dispersed, exiled, and homeless, cowering in ghettos as the rejects of world history. Jesus radicalized even more the view of things from the position of the outsider. He took sides in controversial situations. He placed the kingdom of God in a one-sided relation to those who were getting the worst of it, people who were left out, like those whom our society has called

[6] Jesse Lemisch, "The American Revolution Seen from the Bottom Up," *Towards a New Past: Dissenting Essays in American History,* ed. by Barton J. Bernstein (Random House, 1967), pp. 5-6.

niggers, homos, Commies, Hippies, etc. For could one imagine that Samaritans, prostitutes, publicans, lepers and the demon-possessed held a relatively more advantageous position in Jesus' day?

Student activism is the bad conscience of a Church that has been reading society from the top down. When the Church is allied with power and privilege against *les misérables* in our society, or even refrains from clear advocacy of their cause, she disgraces her calling and needs to be called to repentance. Cataracts have grown over the eyes of ecclesiastics hardened by experience. They become insensitive to the terrific disparity between promises and performance, between rhetoric and reality. The Churches preach a kind of realized eschatology, but they tend to refer all realization to heaven above or to deep down inside. I think student activism has an incarnational thrust; some realization of eschatology is counted on here and now, "on earth as it is in heaven." Theology must become much more practical, that is to say, political. Eschatology is not a sum of transcendental assertions about another world. Rather, it refers to the power of God's kingdom that seeks political actualization under the signature of love and justice. Under our present conditions of life, that is like squaring a circle, or rather more like raising a dead man from the grave. But eschatology cannot give up its links with politics, otherwise it becomes merely an inner feeling of piety or an otherworldly dream. Student activism is a form of praying "Thy kingdom come," however annoying its present-day secular idiom. Many people in the Churches are offended by the life-style of youth activists. As Marcuse says, "the rebellion often takes on weird and clownish forms which get on the nerves of the Establishment."[7] In speaking of the student movement in general, he ascribes to it an "aesthetic morality" which is just the opposite of puritanism. "It does not insist on a daily bath or shower for people whose cleaning practices involve systematic torture, slaughtering, poisoning; nor does it insist on clean clothes for men who are professionally engaged in dirty deals."[8]

Students seem to intuit that they are enlisted in a world liber-

[7] Herbert Marcuse, *An Essay on Liberation*, p. 63.
[8] *Ibid.*, p. 28.

ation movement. They will not often use the symbols of Christian eschatology to articulate their concern. They are tramping around in the world, raising hell for the kingdom of God. They may not know they are doing it for the kingdom, but anyone struggling in solidarity with those whom Jesus called his brethren, hungry and thirsty people, unclothed and sick people, alien and enslaved people, is made to inherit the kingdom of God, according to Matthew 25:31-46. This is the plank on which Christians can stand who find themselves uncomfortably yoked with unbelievers in a solidarity of concern for the oppressed in the world.

III

SCHIZOPHRENICS OF THE KINGDOM

I have been dealing with what student activism can do for the Church and her theology. By pricking the Church's conscience, student activism can move the Church to take sides with people on the bottom, as an imitiation of the one-sidedness of the kingdom of God. And secondly, it can knock theology off its lofty perch of dreary isolation from the suffering world around it, and bring about a new relation between theory and practice by striving for a political grounding of eschatological hope. Theology can then be, in the expression of Ernst Bloch, a "Theorie/Praxis." The activism of theological students is a test in practice whether the theory they learn is true. The truth makes a difference; it is power to change things and action that makes men free.

However, I dare to suggest there are some things that the Church and theology can do for student activism. In the *Chicago Sun-Times,* Michael Harrington had an editorial on the breaking up of the SDS. He pointed out that the student movement is afflicted by a tendency toward ideological abstraction that results in fragmentation. This can only ensure the relative powerlessness of American student movements. The students are imitating their elders in American history, demanding pure doctrine as a condition of fellowship, and quick to pull out and organize a splinter movement around a charismatic personality. This fascination for ideological hair-splitting and personal magnetism is an old, old story in human affairs. It is sad to see the students being taken in.

Andrew Young of the SCLC (Southern Christian Leadership Conference) gave a talk at the "free university" in Cuernavaca, Mexico, in the summer of 1969. He pointed out that the trouble with students is their short-windedness. They get involved in a big campaign for change, but when vacation comes, they're all gone. Again like their elders, they're long on rhetoric, short on deeds. So what is needed, Mr. Young said, are people who think of the movement as their life's calling, who do not think of it as a generational thing, something to do while you're young, but rather a missionary thing, something to do for life. That is where you'll be if you enter the messianic stream of hope that wells up from the future of God in Christ. Messianists are partisans of the future, and therefore cannot be defined by the generational conflict. From the perspective of a qualitatively human vision of the future, there are young people as old as Methuselah and old people who have tapped the source of eternal youth.

This relativizing of the generation gap by the transcending quality of the future that faith in Christ opens up has another dimension to it. It can save students from the self-righteousness to which their zeal and idealism make them prone. Student activism can become a new form of legalism and works-righteousness. When that happens, we have to replay the music of Luther and the Reformation. Student activism can be a syndrome of guilt feelings seeking relief in pure causes, a romantic belief in the innocence of youth, leading to the snobbery about not trusting anyone over thirty, and of a striving for security by keeping up with the last report of where the movement is at. One has to be justified by works, by taking one's lumps, getting arrested, assuming the image of poverty—if not chastity—and faithful adherence to the approved jingoism.

The eschatological perspective brings the judgment of the future also against those who proclaim and promote it in the present. Those who believe in the gospel of the kingdom apply its word of judgment first of all to themselves. This frees them from the delusion of being more pure and guilt-free than others.

Sören Kierkegaard said something to the effect that it is an edifying thought to know that before God we are always in the wrong. The "protestant principle" that Paul Tillich announced with such fervor had the same force of shattering the self-absolutizing tendency that pervades every human venture. The dazzling light of the utopian future often blinds its devotees to the contradictions they embrace in the present. Very often their shrill clamoring for a change in the external conditions of society takes our attention away from the equally great need for a profound change "in the infrastructure of man."[9] There can be no new society without a new type of man, and this can happen, as Marcuse acknowledges, only by way of a transformation in the instinctual nature of man.[10] This awareness can free us from the illusion that just because we entertain beautiful dreams about the future and stand in strong protest against the way things are, somehow we "beautiful ones" have evolved beyond the pale of other mortals and have become already a new species of mankind. The truth is that we are split men and students; we are engaged in a clash between the right of the future to come to pass and the stubborn desire of the present to keep itself intact, and in that clash we become schizophrenics of the kingdom. We pray for the kingdom to come, but we don't want to give way to it in ourselves. The apostle Paul expressed his schizoid condition this way: "For I delight in the law of God, in my inmost self, but I see in my members another law at war with the law of my mind and making me captive to the law of sin which dwells in my members. Wretched man that I am! Who will deliver me from this body of death?" (Rom. 7:22-24) That kept Paul sober and free of boasting about his own importance.

Next to last I would suggest that the student action movement needs a home base. This home base is the Church as the community that celebrates the gifts and graces of life that we now enjoy. There must be times for celebration, for laughing and singing and dancing. There is not only the Iliad of grappling and going down amid the woes of life; there is also the Odyssey of homecoming and taking part in the joyful feasts along the way,

[9] *Ibid.,* p. 5.
[10] *Ibid.,* p. 21.

each of them a mini-snapshot of the crowning fullness of life that awaits us all. We should not let our love for the future cause us to hate the present. We need to sprinkle our seriousness with the salt of humor, lest we imagine that the world can only be saved by our good works.

Finally, a theological seminary can provide space for the mind to explore a society's doubts about itself and to reflect on the wastelands in both the Church and the world into which the servants are sent to minister. The word "seminary" comes from the Latin word "seminarium" meaning "seed-plot" and "semen" means "seed." A seminal idea is one that contains the possibility of future development. Seminarians are supposed to generate such seminal ideas and to plant them in the soil of this world.

PART III

Imaging the Future

9

Appeal to the Person
of the Future

Robert W. Jenson

A conference of *Dialog's* editors both chose "prayer" as the theme
of an issue and moved me to volunteer an article, by what seemed
to me the refusal of some of my colleagues to take prayer for
what it is or leave it alone. The polemical tone of the essay is
essential to it. I am increasingly animated by desire to perceive
the elementary assertions of the gospel for our situation, and the
elementary phenomena of faith in our situation, without the evasions of an unreflecting sophistication. I think also that there is
a two-way relation between this desire and concern for authentic
eschatology: (1) the first concern simply includes the second, and
(2) even the beginnings of labor on the second concern liberate
us for the first. All simple Christian assertions and practices can
be faced only if the fundamental assertion, "He is risen and coming," is not mitigated. Anyway, if the "futurist" theological option is viable, prayer is surely high on the list of matters it must
be able to make sense of. Prayer as "appeal to the future" is not
a new interpretation; prayer as appeal to the *person* of the future perhaps is in some ways.

I

We must start with the elementary phenomena, since it is apparently so easy to ignore them. If we asked someone who had
never before seen people praying to observe us at it and say what
we were doing, he would surely say we were trying to talk to
some entity able to understand and reply to human language, and
that our discourse with this entity covered more or less the whole
range of forms of personal address: information, request, thanks,
etc. If asked, he would surely also say that these forms of our
discourse, together with its usual content, presupposed that we

were at once utterly dependent on this conversational partner, and able to influence him or it.

These are the elementary phenomena. It is therefore exceedingly odd that so many of those who do this praying try to explain their activity in ways that deny these observations. We will be told that the one addressed cannot "really" be influenced, so that the effect of prayer is "really" on the one who prays; e.g., "To pray for peace is to evoke attitudes that will lead to peace." This would seem to imply that prayer is "really" addressed by the worshiper to himself, and even this will often be agreed to. We will hear from some who pray that the point of the enterprise is "really" to break down the line between the prayer and his partner altogether, thus abolishing the situation in which communication, prayer included, makes any sense at all.

It is tempting to say, and let it go at that, that any interpretation of a set of phenomena which must so persistently ignore the obvious has to be perverse—and indeed, so many "really's" are always the sign of the bad kind of philosophizing. More obvious nonsense is probably uttered about prayer by those who do it than in the case of any other human activity; and if the members of many a Christian congregation want to be confused by a string of patent evasions, they need merely question their pastor on the subject. Yet there must be some reason for this tendency of those who pray to explain away their own activity; and an attempt to discern that reason will be the starting point of this article.

We will touch three questions: (1) Why do those who pray regularly interpret their activity so as to make nonsense of it (II)? (2) What difference does the gospel make to this situation (III)? (3) Are there any practical consequences of our answers to (1) and (2) (IV-VI)?

II

Prayer is not peculiar to Christianity; it is perhaps the most universal religious phenomenon. In all religions, the Power which is the fundamental religious reality is experienced pre-eminently in words, in the capacity of words to bind the chaotic given environment to our will for order, and simultaneously to open possibilities beyond the given. Thus all religions also know the special word of Power, the specific blessing or curse or sacramental recital in which the Power works as a reality of our willing existence. Prayer emerges when the Power *in* our word of Power is itself experienced as Will, so that our words are also addressed *to* the Power. It is, therefore, first when prayer emerges that the word of Power is securely established *as word,* as communication. Where prayer does not emerge, or in areas of religious practice where other forms of the word of Power continue to dominate, the position of the word, for all its centrality, is ambiguous: there the word of Power tends to fulfill itself precisely by over-reaching itself as word, by shedding just those semantic characters which distinguish discourse from music or ejaculation, and so at last by returning to silence.

Only in prayer is the word-character of powerful utterance unambiguous. But with the emergence of prayer, the situation becomes unstable in another way. Prayer is a word addressed *to* a Will real for us chiefly *in* that word. Within the usual ontology this situation is precarious. How, we may ask, can a word be addressed to a reality posited in that same word? Thus prayer tends to slip back—often by way of false mystical or psychological sophistication—into the primitive Power-word as such, and then into silence. Where this has happened, where there no longer are robust requests, informations and compliments, but instead perhaps "the burden of a sigh," we are no longer dealing with prayer in any reasonable sense of the word, and should admit it. Thus also analysis of the sighings of such second primitivism is outside the scope of this article.

It is this precarious ontological position which is the ground of our perennial unwillingness to admit the obvious about our praying. Contrary to what is often thought, embarrassment about praying is *not* a modern phenomenon or a phenomenon of secularization. Secularization may close transcendence altogether, in which case one just stops praying. Or—as I will argue—where secularization is interpreted by the gospel, it may free us to pray straightforwardly and without embarrassment. But that we interpret prayer so as to make nonsense of it, without being able honestly to quit the practice, is as old as religion itself. It results from prayer's incomplete emergence from the context of undifferentiated religious Power, where the whole validity of words as words is ambiguous; and it signifies precisely the extent to which we are *not* secularized.

When we think it unworthy of God to be influenced by our addresses, or when we suppose there is no necessity of speaking our will since he already knows it, or when we subscribe to a scientific determinism but continue to posit God, who is thus bound to an impersonal necessity, we posit a God who is not fully personal, who remains in the religious ambiguity between personal will and impersonal *mana*. The very existence of a person is to be affected by others than himself. We speak to God and say "God . . . ," as we might say "John . . . ," but balk the implications of such address. And our hesitancy is not caused by adherence to a modern world-view, but by adherence to the primitive matrix of religion.

III

The gospel verifies the ontological situation of prayer and frees it from religious ambiguity. The touchy point is the *object* of prayer, the entity *toward* whom we speak. Where prayer remains bound to its religious matrix, this object of address tends to vanish, so that the word-situation is falsified. Traditionally we have found—precariously—a way of addressing our prayer by maneuvers like closing our eyes, bowing our heads, and forcing our attention back upon that deep soul to which God's natural affinity might be expected to draw him. Or we have posited a sort of ghost named Jeezuz, resident in certain places and times. We have looked up to the place "heaven." And when we have truly become desperate for an object to which we may address ourselves as we pray, we have oriented to tables, boxes, pictures and antependia.

Secularization has indeed put an end to these devices, except as superstition. Thereby it ought to have freed us to accept what the gospel has always suggested: the present *object, to* which we may direct ourselves as we pray, is the common spirit or joint personality of that community established by our praying words as a communication also between those praying—"Where two or three are gathered in my name. . . . " When we sing our prayer, the music itself accomplishes the direction of our utterance.

Who is this object? How may we identify him or it? We may for some purposes identify it as the "spirit of the congregation" or the like, but if this were the only identification we could make, we would be back with a socialized version of psychologically interpreted prayer to ourselves, and on the way to silence. Instead, we are allowed to identify our object as Jesus of Nazareth— ". . . there am I in the midst of them." An *object* is that *to* which we direct ourselves. It is also that in our experience which can be specified descriptively. We direct ourselves to the word-realized spirit of our community—and descriptively specify this object as Jesus of Nazareth. The *objectivity* of the addressee of our prayer, by which this addressee is an entity other than we, so that the word-situation is authentic, is the historical objectivity, the pastness, of Jesus. The *presence* before us of an entity to which we may address ourselves is the word-reality of our community, the reality between us in which we come together. In one formula we can say: the word-reality of our community mediates the presence of the past object Jesus.

We postpone for one more paragraph the question of how this mediation works in order to consider an objection. Someone might fear that a *mediated* presence of the past Jesus is an inferior presence, that I really am not fully affirming Christ's presence. The answer has three steps. (1) The claim of an unmediated presence of Christ is anyway obviously false—unless we believe in ghosts, we quite evidently do *not* have a "personal relation" to Jesus in any ordinary sense. (2) We have not yet finished a description of all aspects of the godly reality to which we pray, only of the *object* to which we *direct* ourselves in prayer. (3) The presence of *every* object is mediated in one way or another —this insight is the one abiding heritage of Kant's analysis; showing its wider theological importance must be another article.

But what permits us to identify the superpersonal reality of our praying community as Jesus? The first point is that this gathering is "in Jesus' name"; that is, our praying is never the whole of the conversation by which our praying community is constituted; this conversation also has narrative content, and that content is the story of Jesus. Our praying is *response* to other utterances in the same gathering, utterances which bespeak Jesus to the gathering.

This could, of course, mean only the same present mediation of a past reality as that of Caesar in a gathering of historians. Caesar is very really there, but not as will, not as the free partner of a possible and effective discourse on the future of those addressing him. And if not so, then not as the actual past object Caesar, for free personal being is exactly what Caesar objectively was.

If it is different with Jesus, then it is because of a material character of the actual narrative about him: the narrative concludes by asserting that he rose from the dead. The difference between a live man and a dead one is that the dead man opens no more future, whereas we still may expect to be surprised by the freedom of the live one. Thus the narrative about Jesus is a word of promise. It promises us that we will yet be surprised by that freedom enacted in Palestine. And since that freedom was so radical as to work itself out only as self-surrender in death, the narrative about Jesus promises it to us as the future of death, as a final future.

If these promises are true, the past Jesus is also our future destiny—the very destiny we grasp or lose in all our communication with each other. *Therefore* the communal reality created by our communication in Jesus' name can be his presence, and as the presence of the freedom, the person that he—objectively! —was. Our communication promises the free and surprising future act which he will perform; it makes the promise only he can make; thus it claims that he is a *subject* in this conversation, that our communication is his word. If he truly is risen, if he will indeed yet surprise us, this claim is true. And in that case the object posited in our communication is his objectivity.

It is this whole occurrence which is the reality of God, of the specific God of prayer in Jesus' name. We are here involved with God because we are here in a particular way bracketed in time: our last future is the future of the past event Jesus. To be thus bracketed in time is to know eternity, and eternity is the defining character of deity—*how* we are bracketed in time, what sort of eternity occurs, answers which God is real.

So we summarize: *God* is the occurrence of our temporal bracketing by Jesus' freedom. The *objectivity of* God is the historical objectivity of Jesus. The *presence* of that object, so that we may direct ourselves to it, is the superpersonal reality of our word-carried community of narrative and prayer.

The God who occurs as this particular temporal bracketing has emerged wholly from religious ambiguity to be straightforwardly personal. A person is at once an object distinct from other persons, and means free future for them. In the occurrence of bracketing by Jesus' freedom, I have to do with the straightforwardly distinct historical objectivity of Jesus, and just so encounter free futurity of and for my own life.

Not every person, of course, is God. Religiously, the transcendence of the experienced Will is established by uniquenesses which mitigate its personhood: this will is timeless, unaffected by any other will, etc. In total contradiction, the God who occurs as our temporal bracketing by Jesus' freedom is transcendent God precisely by the straightforwardness of his personhood. When we say of a being that it is transcendent, we say two things: (1) it is another entity than we, with the future-posing meaning for us of that otherness, and (2) we cannot overcome this otherness, as we can and do with each other and the things of this world when we deny and close ourselves to one another's freedom. The God of Christian prayer is an other than we as the historical person Jesus was one person and we are others, with the future which is posed us in that conversation in which he is object. And we cannot overcome this otherness, for in the one direction his historical distinction from us has been given the finality of death —without his thereby ceasing to be future for us—and in the other direction that future which he poses is the future *of* death, and so beyond all our devices to shield ourselves from it.

That is, this God's transcendence is an event: the resurrection by which Jesus became the future of our death. Prayer to this God is not, therefore, penetration into a superior level or depth or height of being. It is not a merely personally tinged evocation of Power. It is *appeal to the future*—appeal to the future of Jesus' freedom as the future of all history.

So does the gospel finally verify the situation of prayer, of prayer as—shamefacedly—practiced in every religion. Prayer understood by him who prays as appeal to the future of a straightforwardly objective reality can without inner contradiction be all those things which prayer in any case is. There can be such prayer if there is in fact a God who is the Power of some addressable object's future. According to the gospel, it is just so: God is the Power of Jesus' future. Prayer to him is, unmitigatedly, talk to a person.

IV

Finally, let me draw some direct practical consequences of what I have been saying. First, I have assumed from the beginning that Christian prayer is fundamentally *common* prayer If this assumption is not made, I do not see how Christian prayer can be practiced at all. Apart from the communication between men of the narrative about Jesus, there is no present object to address. The believer is, of course, never apart from this communication; and so he prays also in the physical absence of the congregation. But just as the faith which is at all times the believer's form of life has its home in the telling and hearing of the gospel-story, and so in a gathering, so the believer's "private" prayer is but an extension between times of his common prayer.

Second, prayer is fundamentally an *antiphonal* activity. It is one side of a conversation. The other side is the wide range of utterances—proclamatory narrative, blessing, sacramental formulas, etc.—which bespeak Jesus as the future to those gathered. The ancient formula which introduces many prayers of the traditional liturgies displays the structure in extreme concentration: "The Lord [into this phrase the whole Christian narrative and promise are packed] be with you." "And with you also." "Let us pray."

Third, also our *attention* is antiphonal. The practice of "orienting" during prayer, of facing the gathering all in some one direction (at family prayer, usually down!) so as to face toward God's presence, is utterly inappropriate. It was never appropriate to a specifically Christian self-understanding in prayer; and secularization has in any case made it ridiculous. God is not in that box up there! If he is here at all, his location is *among* us; he is, as it were, at the crossing of the lines of communication between us. So let us look at each other when we pray; or, just possibly, at some marker of the crossing, as at the eucharistic elements at those points in the liturgy where they are the focus of our community-positing communication. And above all, let us "orient" by *listening* to each other.

Fourth, as one side of a conversation with a concrete other side, prayer can, should and does encompass all forms of utterance appropriate to the partner involved. We believe that partner is fully personal, in that he is the Power of a concrete future, the Power of Jesus' future. Therefore, prayer should encompass the full range of personal addresses. None of the forms of address we use to each other need or should be omitted. The difference is the other way around: in addressing me, you must always reckon with the partiality of my freedom. You must use tact, and omit some sorts of address you might use with someone else—perhaps I don't like to be asked for favors. With God, no tact is needed.

V

A fifth point will take more discussion than all the rest. A regular part of our personal discourse with each other, and central to it, are promises and requests, by which I deliver some part of my future to the love of the other. Therefore, promises and requests are appropriate and central also in our talk to God, if God is transcendent precisely by his personhood. Indeed, the joyful making of requests about what is to happen in the future is the very test of Christian prayer; for our prayer *is* appeal to the future. Nor are these to be requests for the sort of future event we really think we might bring to pass ourselves: "Lord, make me more charitable." The heart of Christian prayer is petition for just such futures as are beyond our control, i.e., are in God's control, i.e., are really future: "Lord, let thy kingdom come—and stop the Vietnamese war." Undialectically petitionary prayer is the paradigm of all Christian prayer.

The assertion of the previous paragraph is the inner scandal of this whole discussion. The unbelief in prayer of those who pray most usually comes to expression at just this point. And putting this unbelief into practice by eliminating offensively real petitions is regularly the beginning of prayer's slide through incantation into silence.

Christian prayer begins paradigmatically with "Our Father. . . ." This is to be taken seriously. God's grace is that he permits and encourages our views to be heard and considered in his management of the universe, exactly as the views of no longer infantile children are heard and considered by the father in his management of the household. As a father, I want to hear the opinions of my twelve-year-old daughter, and I reckon with them in making my decisions. The decision remains mine, and I may decide against her; but her expressed opinion is an essential pole of the process of decision. To just this status has God adopted us in Christ: God's household is the universe, and he asks us, his children, what we think should happen in it.

The claim involved in Christian prayer is tremendous, and not likely to be believed by many. To pray is to lay claim to co-determination of the universe. But no lesser status would make prayer worth bothering with at all. Nor is it arrogance to utter petitions and so take up this claim. On the contrary, to cast ourselves on our Father with our petitions is exactly the sort—the only sort—of humility appropriate before the gospel's God. The sort which is too humble to trouble God is phony—for it is in fact a disguise for unbelief in God's reality as free love, and for the correlated insistence that I will handle my own life for myself, and what I can't deal with I will leave to impersonal fate.

If, of course, God does not in fact freely manage the universe, petitionary prayer can't work—but then neither is any other form of Christian prayer meaningful, for then there isn't the Christian God. Yet so abrupt a dismissal of this scruple would be unhelpful, for a regular hindrance to prayer is undoubtedly the feeling that the orderliness of the world, as the sciences investigate it, precludes particular free acts of governance by God in response to our prayer. Only the barest sketch of a therapy for this scruple can be offered here.

In the course of Western culture, reality has fallen apart into two realms. There is "nature," which we posit by predicting events from laws and boundary conditions; and there is "history," which we posit by interpreting events with words like "future" or "decision." Under condition of the separation of these realms, the success of the scientific enterprise seems to require a deterministic interpretation of nature, while the very point of history is the posit of the possibility of freedom.

The separation once accomplished, we find we cannot maintain it; for every event belongs to both realms. We may correctly insist that every event may be both explained by scientific prediction and interpreted as history, and that these two understandings do not clash; but we are not satisfied to let it go at that. If now we subsume history into deterministically understood nature, we do indeed derive an interpretation of the world's transformations through time in which divine governance would be unfitting. But to believe in a free God is to believe that reality is the other way around, that nature is a particular, and useful, abstraction from history. Nor is there anything in the methods, ethos or results of the sciences that would fight this interpretation; though the task of producing it in detail by, for example, interpreting relativity theory's "time" in terms of historical "time," is probably at present beyond anyone's capacity.

Even in such a world, the governance of a *theos* metaphysically outside the world would be interference. But the God to whom Christians pray is the Power of an historical event's future. If real at all, he is in no sense "outside" the historical world. The event in question is such, we have seen, that if it has a future it must be the *last* future. Thus the Power of this future, if real at all, is the openness to the future in which *every* event occurs, is every event's *own freedom*. Since this freedom of every event is the freedom of Jesus, of a person, we can appeal to it. We can *appeal to* the freedom of the events of our lives, and that is what we do when we pray.

VI

A sixth and last consequence draws the most important facet for the life of today's Church. Prayer accomplishes things. It is in part work: in the world on the world's future. When we pray for someone, we intend thereby to accomplish something for him. Prayer is that particular part of man's work on his and his world's future which is left up to the believers in God. It isn't the whole of their share of man's task, but it is the part that only they can do. Nor, of course, is this work the whole of their prayer; some of prayer is play, for prayer embraces the whole range of possible personal conversation.

Even when we don't feel like playing, the work is still to be done. When believers understand themselves, they gather on some regular plan to pray, with a list of things that need doing in the world. They gather when their religious needs or inner faith draw them, and they also gather when they don't—just as with the other parts of their work in the world. And they leave with the assurance of a job done—not the only job, but a useful one. Past this observation, there is nothing more to say except "Let us pray"—and that can't be said in print.

10

Worship as Drama

Robert W. Jenson

This essay was written for *Janus,* the journal of the Roman Catholic student movement in Oxford. The assertions made about worship are intentionally platitudinous; the reasons suggested for the necessity of these assertions perhaps are not. Cult is the area where religion and the gospel are most directly united and most influentially at odds. Therefore interpretation of our worship in terms of the particular temporal modalities granted by the gospel is especially pressing, both for the theological enterprise exhibited in this volume and for our stifled and stifling worship.

I

All consideration of the relation between Christian worship and the rest of human culture must begin with the fact of the basic liturgical art: the drama. Worship *is* a dramatic performance. Why this is so is our topic; that it is so is empirically evident. What we in fact do as the central act of our worship would necessarily be described by an innocent observer so: one of them plays Jesus and the rest play disciples, and they act out that bit of Jesus' story about their last meal together.

The other arts occur in worship incidentally to its dramatic character, and for the same reasons as they occur in the drama generally. This performance occupies a stage, and uses stage-settings, costumes, props, and above all rhythmically and melodically intensified language. Therefore the poets, musicians, goldsmiths, painters, designers, architects, and all the troop of art are called in to work on the production. And if they are not, if the play is done in "everyday language" and in "modern dress" or rehearsal clothes, this too is an artistic device for a particular effect. All this must be worked out in depth, but our present task is the prior one: *Why* is worship intrinsically dramatic?

II

The Christian Church—whatever may be true of other worshiping communities—is the community of a particular narrative communication, of a story. It is that gathering which occurs when one man tells others the gospel-story. This is the story of what happened with Jesus the Israelite, told as a story which concerns the teller and his hearers ultimately. It is the story of a figure from the *past,* told as the last *future,* as the story of what is finally to come of our lives, as a promise of the fulfillment that will make sense of what we have suffered, done and been. The Church's worship is simply the total of what happens on such occasions of gospel-communication.

Many will want to say other things of the Church and her worship, and some of these will be controversial. Our definition is offered as a non-controversial minimum. The problem of this paper is: Why must our gatherings around the gospel-story be dramatic performance of the story and not its mere telling? Why do we celebrate the eucharist instead of just having a reading of Mark 14?

III

I take it that one thing that distinguishes a drama from a mere narration is dialogue: a drama is dialogical narration. So is the gospel.

On the one hand, the telling of the gospel is a live moral and existential challenge made by one person to another. It is the challenge to a new possible mutual future made here and now by you to me and me to you, and must be such a confrontation to be the gospel at all. For it is the very point of the gospel that it is news, and surprising news, that it must be told *to* me, that I cannot know it in advance of hearing it. The gospel is the word that frees me from bondage to the past, from guilt and hopelessness, and opens a future. But this word I cannot speak to myself— for I would speak it in the course of my old life, the life I already have, and just so close myself to its message. Freedom from my past for our future can only be *given* me by someone else who brings me news that I could not anticipate. And so the gospel is an event *between* persons, a mutual challenge to freedom and responsibility.

Were this all that were to be said of the gospel, the category of language-activity into which it fits would be that of conversation. But unlike a conversation, the gospel has a necessary narrative content which is given prior to our exchange, which is laid down in advance and is not the creation of our moment. We have a text to recite. And this of course is just what we need, if we are to free each other in our words. The gospel must be news —for *both* of us. Therefore, while the gospel is conversation, it on the other hand remains what we called it at the beginning: *narrative*.

We put the two together: the gospel is a conversation which is also a fixed narrative. That is, it is dramatic *dialogue*—which is what we wanted to prove.

In a way, this is true of any story—if it is interesting enough to tell at all. Any such story will be at once future-opening, that is, conversational, and narrative. And indeed, we regularly experience the impossibility of telling any really good story without acting it out, without gesture and role-imposed voice changes. But the gospel is that story which is not only future-opening, but an explicit promise of that future *to* which we may be opened. Thus this particular story cannot be told non-dramatically at all: the story of Jesus and Israel set down in books, and perhaps read, is not the gospel.

IV

There is, I think, a further usual difference between mere narration and drama. The case of radio drama shows that we are willing to call drama language-activities which meet no further specifications than being dialogical. But we usually feel radio drama as a limiting case; and we think of drama as properly involving seeing as well as hearing, as involving *gesture* in the broadest sense. If we ask why we feel this way, we will find another reason why Christian worship must be dramatic.

Drama involves seeing as well as hearing because the *body* is essential to drama and the body is seen rather than heard. To be sure, the voice is also—if we stop to think—a bodily phenomenon: if a speaker were to lose his body he would not merely no longer be seen, he would also lose the ability to make himself heard. And yet somehow an audible disembodied spirit seems plausible, whereas a visible spirit requires exactly a materialization. Scientifically, the voice is a bodily phenomenon; but when we contrast body with spirit, words belong to the spirit and visibility to the body.

One more step completes this part of the argument. The body is our *identifiability* to each other. My presence to you in language alone—as in this paper—is ambiguous as to *who* is present—except perhaps by "tone," that is, by the most bodily side of our words. When we want to know who is speaking, we try to get a look at the face or figure. So: in dialogue we want to identify each other; therefore we want bodily presence. The body is seen and not heard; therefore in dialogue we want to see.

We have still not, however, gotten to *gesture*. We do not find it dramatic to see the immobile body; it is the body in *motion* that is dramatic. This is explicable by yet another consideration: my body represents my *past,* for it is by my past that I am identifiable. If I say, "Jones is reliable," and you ask, "Who is Jones?" I will have to respond by saying, "Jones is the one who married Nancy Smith, who works for Hinshaw's, who . . . ," and continue with such "who . . ." clauses until you identify Jones. Notice that the content of all these "who . . ." clauses will be information about the past. Jones' body, as the presence of the identifiable Jones, represents his past. If, in dialogue, we want to see the body move, this means that we want to see *the past move*—the movement of the past is what drama seeks to bring to pass.

Drama is thus that mode of the word which explicitly calls us into history, into that transcendence of the future which breaks the frozen immobility of the past; *therefore* it uses gestures, and not only sound- or print-born words. Drama is that mode of the word which not only presupposes and enacts temporal transcendence, but has temporal transcendence as its theme. In drama remembrance and hope come together. In drama *what* is said, and the future-opening which with any living communication is the *saying* of it, coincide. Therefore the drama is the form of word demanded by the gospel. The gospel is that message which calls us into history, which as the tale of a figure from the past opens a future unbound by the past. The gospel is the promise of that temporal transcendence which is the theme of drama.

V

Therefore it is too weak to say that the drama is the form "demanded by the gospel." There is, so long as we remain within our present purely formal mode of description, no way to distinguish between drama and gospel at all.

In fact, not every drama is the gospel—far from it. But if the gospel is true, then we must indeed be willing to say that there is finally only one text which is not beyond our performing. With all other texts we are driven to hire special actors to perform *for* us, who are able to carry their roles just because they have cut themselves off from the community. The gospel we can perform ourselves—and if we find the Church doing her worship as performance by special actors for a congregation that has become an audience, this is the surest sign there can be that the Church has forgotten the gospel and adopted an alien dialogue.

It further follows that not only is all Christian worship drama, but all drama is worship—the only question being: Which God is being worshiped? Nor is this merely the familiar genetic point. Even the secularized drama of the modern West is worship, worship of the hidden God. For a God is one who in some way reconciles past and future; all drama is therefore divine revelation.

VI

Let me conclude with some exhortations. The point is not that the liturgy should be done with dramatic embellishments, or even "dramatically." The simple meal around someone's kitchen table may well be the form of eucharist best celebrated by men like us. The point is that the liturgy *is* a drama, of which we are the actors—and that it is a drama by the very nature of the gospel. Theologically: there can be no gospel without sacraments, yet neither are the sacraments an addition to the proclamation; they are the acting-out side of the proclamation, without which the proclamation itself does not occur.

The conclusion that worship is drama is not new; it could not be, since—as we said at the beginning—it is simply an obvious fact. But perhaps the argument which has led to this obvious proposition is in some ways novel. And perhaps some benefit might come ecumenically from a new line of reasoning at this point. For it is above all the *reasons* which Roman Catholics have given for the dramatic character of worship which have offended Protestants and been responsible for what Protestants must judge to be the distortions of Roman Catholic worship. Vice versa, the lack of any better reasons, of insight into why worship must be sacramental to be evangelical, has led Protestants into trying to evade the obvious by expunging the dramatic character of worship—thereby transforming it into something else altogether: dogmatic lecture, moral uplift meeting, or sociological seminar.

Perhaps if we were to start again at the beginning, with the simplest observations and the most elementary analysis, we would be able to work together to a better understanding and practice of worship than either group has at present. This paper has been the beginning of one such attempt.

11

God, Space and Architecture

Robert W. Jenson

Originating as a section-paper for the 1966 conference of the Lutheran Society for Worship, Music and the Arts, the essay was subsequently published in *Response*. Rather impassioned affirmative and negative replies from architects demonstrated both the promise and the danger of attempting to revamp the theological interpretation of any part of life that makes a difference to someone. The three essays, of which this is the second, should be read together as bits and pieces of the esthetic eschatology postulated in Chapter V.

Church architecture, to put it tritely, is the definition of spaces that are to be used for gatherings to worship God. Our question is: What sort of spatial definition does this activity require? This question obviously presupposes the motto, "Form follows function," but in the broad sense in which it is *a priori* true it serves mostly to raise further questions about the spatiality of the "function" in question. In the present case, considerations such as what sort of liturgy must be provided for or how many must be able to participate can be taken care of quite quickly and leave most of the important decisions unsettled: shall the lines of the building be parallel, convergent, radial? what should be the shape of the floor plan? should the design be harmonious and restful, or dissonant and nervous? should the surfaces be richly decorated or bare? To deal with these problems we must take up the question really posed by "Form follows function" and ask: Why does worshiping God need a space? In what sense is the relation of worshipers to God a spatial relation? To deal with these questions we must deal with some apparently remote reflections, which can here only be asserted in thesis-fashion. If we will stick with them they will, however, lead straight back to architecture.

God enters our lives with the question posed by time, better, by the temporality, indeed the mortality, of human life. Because I have a future, because I not only am what I am but will be what I will be, I am always asked what will become of me— asked by family, profession, chance meetings, and myself. And because the only certain future is death, which is my cessation, I cannot dispose once for all of my future, and so cannot bring its question to silence. That is to say, I cannot answer it myself— which is the entry of God into my life.

I

The question of the spatiality of our relation to God is, there-fore, the question of how we move in space as we try to deal with the question posed by time. But what is space to time? Space is precisely the present as against the past and the future. Space is precisely that in which things are present, are now to me. Space is that in which presence occurs. The things in space are those which are now there for me, which neither no longer are nor not yet are.

One possible way of facing the challenge of the future to what I already am, of facing the threat of the future, is to use that which is now, which is presently at hand, to secure myself against the threat of the future. I can use space, the accessibility of things which are now, to defend myself against time, the uncertainty of what may come. This is the classical course of the man who built his barns and stored his goods, who used structures and what they could contain of things present to his hand, in order to be able to say to himself, "Soul, you have ample goods laid up for many years; take your ease, be merry." I can do this because things presently at hand in space are assured: there the thing is, and I can be certain at least of that. Thus if I define reality as presence, if I live by the maxim that what is real is what is here and now, what is in space, I can dismiss the threat of the

future as unreal fantasy. I can assure myself against the doubtful and questioning future by what is assured, by what is in my
barns or in my telescope.

There is, of course, a notorious hitch to this, pointed out by
the parable. We cannot escape that we have a future. What we
do, therefore, is to seek to broaden the present at the expense of
the future, to expand the space of time which is assured and
accessible and in our control. This is what the man with his barns
was about. It is what technology is about. But then we discover
that within this broadened present the threat of time reap-
pears: moth and rust corrupt the contents of our barns; the
present things we rely on decay and become obsolescent, and so
do we.

Thus the final solution is to posit an unassailably present being, a being who already is all that it will be and therefore has
no future to threaten us, a changeless and therefore a pure and
perfect presence. This is the solution of religion—and the God
of religion is therefore the Absolute Presence. His mode of life
is the *nunc simul,* the all-ready-now-at-once of eternity. For him
the future is already now, there is no not-yet, and in him therefore we have a present being, something now there, who is our
perfect guarantee against all threats from the future.

To be sure, in order to be changeless God must not be condi-
tioned by the relations which exist between things in space. Everything in space changes—this is the discovery which leads us to
posit God in the first place. The God of religion is therefore not
conceived as a thing in space. But he is experienced as the one
in whom we find what we vainly seek in things in space as the
fulfillment of spatiality. He is the posit of the existential meaning of space. Our relation to him is therefore experienced analogously to spatial relations: we experience his presence, his
being now for us, as nearness, and his transcendence, the
unassailability of his presence, as distance.

Finally to the point: spaces which are defined for the worship
of this God can provide spatially for the relation of the worshipers to the object of their worship. The transcendence of God
can be provided for by establishing a distance, the nearness of
God in worship by arranging this distance as one which is in

some way overcome in the action of worship. Distance and its over-coming combine when the structure also establishes a direction to the *place* where God is.

Distance between the worshipers and God is most directly pro-vided by building two separated locations, one the location of the worshipers, the other the location of the Presence—with some sort of back-and-forth between these locations as what is done in worship to experience God's nearness. The Gothic pattern of nave and choir comes immediately to mind. But the principle was well established long before Gothic times, and despite Protestant trumpetings about tearing down rood screens and so on, the prin-ciple is followed still in almost all church building, Protestant or Catholic—only of course in vulgarized form: Catholics have built holy theaters for viewing the sacred act, with the stage up front as the location for the Presence and an auditorium for the worshipers; Protestants have built holy lecture halls for hear-ing the sacred discourse, with the lecture-desk as the holy place up there and with sound rather than sight as the bridge between the two locations; and Lutherans have made a clumsy combina-tion of the two.

This arrangement automatically also establishes a direction to God—forward to the altar or pulpit. This direction can then be architecturally emphasized in the most various ways: by colon-nades, strong lines that converge in perspective, etc. The simplest way is to shape the building as one or another polygon and put the furniture and props of worship in one angle or against one side so that when people worship, one focus of the building necessarily becomes the focus of their attention. The very crudest is to make the building rectangular and jam altar, pulpit and font, and whatever decoration there is all against one short side. This is the most popular method with modern church architec-ture, in which Protestants stubbornly persist even now when Rome is abandoning it.

The distance to God is architecturally definable also by one or another vastness of the structure so that the defined space reaches out beyond that occupied by the worshipers. This vastness can be quite diffuse, as in Worms Cathedral, or St. Paul's. Or it can be combined with direction, as in the great Gothic churches where the vastness reaches upward and forward. In Gothic churches the structure itself draws us through God's distance to his presence. Gothic architecture synthesizes all the means we have discussed for providing spatially for the God of religion; it is the perfect religious architecture, and our hankering for it in religious moments is a sound, if reprehensible, intuition.

II

It will, I trust, have been divined that my intent is polemic against this apprehension of God and against the architecture which provides spaces designed for worshiping God as so apprehended. Every great age of the Church makes its peculiar discovery about the gospel: the discovery of our age is that the God about whom the gospel speaks is not simply the same as the God of religion—indeed, that he is his antithesis. This discovery is omnipresent in the theology of all confessions and schools. It is therefore all the more remarkable that it has had so little effect on the appurtenances of our faith, including our architecture. I suggest that a main cause of the universally admitted emptiness of our worship is that we persist in building and using structures in which it is impossible to worship any other God than the God of religion in whom the gospel no longer permits us to believe.

The gospel calls forth a way of living that is the opposite of religion. For faith it is precisely the threat of the future, the possibility of the new and different which separates me from what I already have and am, which gives me my true self. This is the life given by a word like "Rise up and walk," which detaches me from security in what I already am and precisely so gives me hope. This is the life given by the word of forgiveness, which tells me I may forget the past and its determination of the present and live for the future. The gospel makes of the present the moment of decision, an act of commitment of the past to the future. Things presently at hand become opportunities for decision. And so space becomes the arena of meeting such opportunities.

In the pattern of life evoked by the gospel, God, far from being our posit to defend ourselves from the challenge of the future, is the challenger, the speaker of the word which detaches us from the status quo and lets us live for what is coming. The God of religion is the absolute and changeless Presence. In direct antithesis, the God of the gospel is the coming one.

The present reality of this God, his being *now* for us, is therefore not a quasi-spatial nearness but rather the *event* of this word which opens the future being spoken. The God of the gospel does not now exist, analogously, to things in space; he happens. Worship of this God is not a relation to a Presence out or up or in there; it is a relation to the future. The overcoming of the separation from God which occurs in prayer and praise is not an appeal to a distant one but to a coming one. And his present is not a presence, but the occurrence of the word of the gospel being spoken between us, the occurrence of our telling each other the story of Jesus as the story of our joint destiny, and of our acting that story out as we do so (the sacraments).

It is plain that we cannot provide spatially for the relation of worshipers to this God by distance and direction. For this God's separation from us, his transcendence, is temporal and not spatial. And his present is exactly what we do, so that his space is not a different space from the one we occupy as we worship him.

The space provided for the worship of this God, for his present, must be a space for this action, for the telling and acting-out of the gospel. It must, that is, be wholly a stage. And there must be no auditorium, for here there are no spectators; here the telling and acting-out is not done for the worshipers but between the worshipers; here the place of God is not a different place from that of the worshipers.

III

As with any good stage, the arrangement of the furniture to be used for the action should be completely flexible. For reasons which we will see in a moment, the best everyday arrangement will probably be central, with the table in the center, but it should be possible to clear this away at a moment's notice. It is not possible to decree in advance a changeless staging for any drama, and once it is recognized that the entire church building is a stage, with no auditorium, all basis for a permanent interior distinction of locations is gone.

The definition of the space to be used for worship should turn all lines back on the volume of space used by the worshipers, rather than away from it. It should direct us not to a holy location but precisely to each other. The whole idea of a common focus for all present is exactly what we must overcome in our church architecture. For God's present is exactly the moment of our action; his space, therefore, is the space that action takes up. A space for worship is the capsule of a moment.

IV

The otherness of the God of the gospel is the otherness of the future. Thus it cannot be comprehended by a space, whether by distance within that space or by a direction of that space. Rather, the otherness of the God of the gospel means that the moment of decision and action for which a defined space provides a capsule has its meaning only in what will come of it, only in another moment future to it: i.e., the otherness of the God of the gospel means that the space used to worship him, the space of the moment of decision and action, is not complete in itself and must not appear to be. Its forms should, therefore, be broken, restless, even nervous. The Renaissance ideal of harmony, of the creation of a space which allows us to rest content in the given moment, is here what must be overcome. We should not find a church soothing. The forms of church buildings should be ready to fall, or to take wing. They should have the dynamics of the temporary.

It is clear that these last considerations suggest that spaces defined for worship should be small. What about large congregations? Quite possibly this question will be answered by the disappearance of large congregations, as the full consequences of the end of Christendom work themselves out. Surely the erection of great buildings designed to stand a thousand years is now a most dubious undertaking. But if large churches are to be built, then perhaps the temporality of the moment of worship may be established by making them so diffusely large that any one gathering within them will seem an encampment from and to which to wander.

The life of faith, the life of such tellings and enactings of the story of Christ, is itself a story: I proceed from one such enactment to another, and this succession has a plot established by the distinction of baptism, preaching, and eucharist. Thus the relation between the parts of the life of worship is temporal and not spatial. Therefore, instead of defining one space for all parts of the life of worship, and then distinguishing and relating them spatially by putting the altar here, the pulpit there, and the font in a third location, there should be several rooms for various purposes, so that as we worship we go from one to another. How far this could be carried out would vary with circumstances, but surely the original custom of separate baptistries should be reestablished.

V

Finally, the space for worship is the space for the enacting of a particular story, the story of Jesus as the story in which the worshipers may find their destiny. On this stage it is always the same play that is performed. But the structure as such cannot establish this; only what, for want of a better term, we call the decoration can provide the scenery which defines the space as one set up for enactment of this particular drama. As we live in a church building the story of Jesus of Nazareth should surround us, in sculpture, fresco, stained glass, mosaic, etc. The passion for bareness of much modern church architecture was a necessary purge of cheap and irrelevant decoration, but is inherently inappropriate to the purpose, for a bare church is too undetermined as to which God is to be worshiped. Nor should such didactic decoration be limited to a few areas, for this would again establish a holy focus. Rather, the eye and even the body should be led to make journeys of exploration through a church building, discovering here a crucifix, there a healing miracle.

These reflections may be accused of utopianism, with good reason. Yet it is surely realism to recognize that in contemporary architecture we have not yet found even partly satisfactory forms for spaces for worship. We have continued to build for a religious Christianity which has long since gone hollow. It is the want of theological reflection on what sort of space God in fact takes that is the main cause of this failure.

12

Worship as Word and Tone

Robert W. Jenson

This essay was one of a series of lectures on "Theological Esthetics" given at Oxford in the spring of 1968, and is printed here to fill out a sort of unit that developed naturally. Like the previous essay, it is an attempt at phenomenology of one side of human life, with theological commitments in the background (I would argue that this is always true of phenomenology). Because of the commitments, such analyses can if desired function directly as critical-theological examination of the life of the Church, and do so here.

According to a dictum of Schleiermacher, the proper vehicle of religion is the tone rather than the word—and he is surely right. Through all periods and cultures music has been the invariable artifact of worship. The attempt of this essay will be to interpret this connection so as, perhaps, to illumine the role of music in the life of specifically Christian worship and of Christian faith.

I

It is impossible to draw any clear *a priori* line between speech and song; the line can be drawn only pragmatically and for a given language and linguistic situation. When we speak of the syntax, semantics, melody and rhythm of a sample of language, we are only analyzing aspects of the concretely indivisible articulation by which that body of sound functions as language. The audible phenomena of articulation are themselves even partly interchangeable in function: thus sequential variation of pitch, which in some languages is usually detachable melody, has regular semantic function in other languages and syntactic function in yet others.

Apart from advanced technology, sound is the only body which is so variously and indefinitely articulable by us; it is therefore the destined chief material for artifacts made as communication. All important points follow from such mundane facts as that while we reflect and do not emit light, we emit and do not significantly reflect sound, and that technological improvement of the capacity to emit sound (musical instruments!) is both earlier and simpler than technological creation of an ability to emit light. The ontologically fundamental consequences are that sound is experienced as a body extended in time rather than in space, and indefinitely malleable at our will.

Thus articulated sound is a medium which extends through time as our life extends, and the pattern of whose temporal extension is in our control. It can move with us through time; it runs along with the temporal self-transcendence of historical existence. It is therefore the literally fundamental language. And religion—which is our attempt to master our temporality and fulfill its transcendence—depends utterly on this language. Before it is anything else, religion is a matter of articulating sound.

II

But what of Schleiermacher's saying, which distinguishes the word from the tone—i.e., one set of aspects of speech's articulation from another set—and gives religious priority to the second? We may think of a spectrum of utterance from, perhaps, mathematically formalized scientific prose read in a monotone and monorhythm, at one extreme, to a Bach partita at the other. At either extreme we are close to a limit of language. What happens as we move along the spectrum is that to modes of articulation which have in the broadest sense semantic function, i.e., which occur at the meeting of an utterance with reality transcendent to the utterance, non-semantic articulations are added. Then the semantic articulations drop out and are replaced by these others. We would reach the far limit of language with pure music: a richly articulated speech no longer wishing to be *about* anything at all, which was meaningful without needing to mean any reality transcendent to itself.

This way of distinguishing music, as an aspect of all utterance, is very abstract. Whether any actual music is "pure" in the sense above may be doubted, but, fortunately, resolving that doubt is irrelevant to my point. What is given in reality is an array of utterances; this array is *orderable* as a spectrum from—probably non-occurring—pure discourse to—equally unlikely—pure music by the abstract distinction I have tried to state. In the following, this abstract use of "music" must be always in mind. It should also be noted that I have given no way of telling one piece of music from another, and will not in this essay. My distinction by no means serves a general understanding of music; it serves only my present narrow purpose.

Even abstractly, pure music would be speech, and the musical aspects of all speech's articulation belong to its reality as communication. But what does music communicate? It does not communicate meanings, for every meaning is the meaning *of* something. I suggest that music rather communicates the sheer possibility of meaning, the mere and all-encompassing occurrence of our self-transcendence. What we share through music is not this or that thought or attitude, but rather the miraculous possibility of thought and attitude. Specification of particular meanings is the work of semantic articulations of sound; it is the work of words rather than of tones.

Speech is the articulated body which can accompany our temporality and in which we therefore can share that temporality. Speech is the articulated body which can accompany our meaning, our projection of ourselves onto a future, and in which we share that future. By our words we share the specification of our future; by the music of our utterance we share our futurity itself. Every address of one man to another is some sort of promise or threat; it calls in one way or another to hope or despair. To make music is to hope for or despair of hope itself, to confront the future utterly without remembrance and so without any particular object of hope. Really "pure" music would have the function Bultmann attributed to the gospel: openness to sheer futurity as such. And it is by the music of *any* utterance that it can be whatever sort of challenge of the future it is.

Of course, melodic or rhythmic patterns which are first musical can also become, in effect, words. Indeed, whole modes of music can acquire specific attitudinal or even literary meanings; and composers can deliberately create or use these increments to write music which expresses particular meanings. When this is done, it is the same as if the music were written to a text. And the musical elements so used acquire and fulfill semantic functions in exactly the same ways as any other words or phrases.

I think, however, that much less of this happens than is sometimes supposed. I am sure there are no particular sorts of meanings especially adapted to be carried by semantically functioning music, e.g., "emotions." And I am very skeptical whether any musical modes or patterns intrinsically carry certain meanings; but it is not important to my argument to assert this.

What I do want to insist is that such specific meanings are not the peculiar sort of meaning which the musical articulation of a sung text, and it alone, brings to the text, or which is the essential and unique communication of textless and programless music. Music's own special meaning is rather the openness into the future in which all particular meanings occur, the mere possibility of promise or threat as such.

If religion is our attempt to deal with the futurity of our existence, it is already apparent why the musical articulation of our communication is essential to religion in a special way. But it is not yet apparent why religion should strive to posit a distinction, and then a separation, between word and tone, so as to locate itself in tone. To see this, we must note that religion is a *particular* way of dealing with our temporality. Religion experiences the openness of the future as a threat, and tries to assuage this threat of temporality by positing eternal Being "beyond" or "above" or "at the depth of" temporal reality. In this Being, there is no not-yet to be threatening; there the future is already now in the divine *nunc simul*.

Done in the context of cult, music provides just this *nunc simul*. On the one hand, it is the language of abstract futurity. On the other hand—and only at first thought is this paradoxical—as the semantic functions of utterance fade, utterance is more noticed simply as sound, more perceptible merely as a body. It presents itself more as a thing available in the present, as an item of what already is. Thus the music of our utterance both is the evocation of futurity and is for us the present and defined bodiliness of our communication. Music can be the reality of futurity as an item of the present, which thus becomes an eternal present—and it is just this for which religion seeks. Thus music *is* the religiosity of discourse: the action by which we participate in divine being, the side of our communication by which it can be communication of the gods.

Thus, for example, in the Upanishads the first creation is a middle realm, which is still eternity but also already time, and which thus mediates our flight from time to eternity. This realm is a world made of music: its substance is tone and its articulation is melody and rhythm. Cult is participation in this realm; therefore the music-sacrifice is the main sacrifice, and the sacred cave or deliberately cave-like temple is fundamentally a resonator. Indeed, the sacrifice of music has even cosmologically redemptive efficacy; the material world and its individualized gods are frozen music, and the music-making of worship frees the gods' melody, liberating them to their impersonal deity and the world from its materiality.[1]

III

Neither textless music, nor musicless discourse can, therefore, be at the center of Christian worship. Probably, of course, neither ever actually occurs: discourse always has some non-semantic articulation, and any actual music will use elements which have picked up semantic function. But utterance can strive toward either limit; neither striving is appropriate to the language-event which is the communal reality of the Church. For the gospel is the story of Jesus told as the promise of our last destiny. As

[1] For endless examples of this sort, see the works of Martin Schneider, most conveniently his article in *RGG3,* Bd. IV, Sp. 1197-1201.

promise of our destiny, it is utterance that opens the future; it requires—or rather, first justifies—the musical articulation by
which our utterances can be utterances of hope. But it is a *specific* promise, deriving its specificity from its determined narrative content as talk about Jesus of Nazareth. It therefore requires
the semantic articulation by which sound mediates particular
meanings.

All specificity of meaning is obtained by reference of utterance
to temporal reality. Just so, specificity of meaning impedes religion. Religion seeks its harmony of past and future in a *timeless*
eternity beyond or above this temporal reality, and therefore not
by a word which is in any essential way about historical contents.
A final promise as an historical narrative is a word of "religion
against itself."

The Church has long experience of unbroken religion's coun-
ter-attack, of the attempt in her own life to flee from the world
as it is and live in the future as the (eternal) present. The
Church's judgment on this attempt has always been the same as
when Paul encountered it at Corinth: we are not yet at the end, and
the very reality of that future end depends upon this not-yet and
its specificity. When religious forces appear in the Church which
can find expression only in meaningfulness without specific meaning, in music without words or pure religious beauty generally,
the Church suspects another such attempt is in progress.

When textless music—or purely decorative visual arts or abstract dance—claim an *independent* place as *language* in the
Church, they are the gnostic enthusiasm which seeks liberation
from the facts of time in a present eternity. The phenomenon is
old; in the primitive Church it appeared as speaking in tongues.
Tongue-speaking was language at its own border, language which
detached itself from shared rules of articulation, and so from any
semantic functions of its articulation, from any need or ability
to be *about* anything. As prayer, it was *pure* "I-Thou" confrontation, saying nothing about either partner. It was the language
of angels, of beings we are not, a linguistic experience of life
in present fulfillment alone. Textless music in the Church and
art without literary content generally are the sophisticated replacement for tongue-speaking.

Paul saw value in tongues. He said that a believer might indeed so press toward consummation of his fellowship with the Lord as from time to time to lose linguistic hold of the world as it is. Yet whatever such eschatological utterance might mean in the experience of the believer, one thing it could not be: it could not be that sharing of a common world by which the Church could live in communication about the man Jesus and the promise of a specific destiny contained in his story. So also the hearing of a Mozart sonata may very well be a decisive and necessary event in the history of my personal life of faith, perhaps the very birth-movement of longing for fulfillment. But when I and my fellow believer sit and listen together to that sonata, each of us lives his own life. The common world of history in which we and Jesus of Nazareth are items, and in which he and I can come to understanding about him, is just what we permit each other for the moment to ignore.

If there was to be tongue-speaking in the life of the community, said Paul, let it be interpreted, let its content-less transcendence be pinned to subsequent words. Likewise we may say: By all means let there be, when we gather, an organ-piece to lift us each to longing for his private heaven. But let it be interpreted; let it be a hymn-prelude which is then given gospel-meanings by the text of the hymn which follows. Believing music will be the music of informative and specifically promising discourse, of assertions that can be right or wrong. Pure musical worship would be the enthusiastic cult of gnostic deity.

On the other hand, the drive to eliminate from worship's utterance the musical aspects of utterance's articulation is an equal disaster. Its success would be the triumph of *moralism*. If our mutual address does not communicate what the musicality of every address communicates, the very possibility of a future, it cannot make the gospel-promise, no matter what it says.

The whole of worship is utterance, and therefore in some degree musically articulated in every part. But at those points in our worship where we most strain forward to the fulfillment of the story we are mutually telling, it is appropriate that musical articulations become more dominant, that we move from "saying" to "singing."

Indeed, at some points song is not merely appropriate, but urgent. Such acclamations as "therefore with angels and archangels and with all the company of heaven we laud and magnify thy glorious name" in the traditional liturgy, make very little sense of any sort when merely spoken. Angels and archangels, to say nothing of the unspecified others, are not the sort of beings we prosaically count to the number of our praying company, like cooks and policemen, and were never thought to be. But when sung, the passage goes perfectly well. One might even suggest that the music itself is the reality of the angels and archangels in question.

As worship becomes prosy, its utterance loses those articulations by which it can free us from the status quo of our lives and world, by which it can function as promise. Then the specific futures once held out as hope and promise become mere ideals, and our realization of them mere tasks. Our worship becomes a moralistic exercise.

The Swiss Reformation and its consequences are an obvious case. But today the authors of "experimental" orders of liturgy are equal sinners. Experiment is obviously and properly prompted by the perception that something essential is missing in our worship. But so blinded have we become to the true nature of worship's language that experimenters regularly assume that what is missing is conceptual clarity. When we "translate" into more "contemporary" and explanatory language, without profound reflection on the varied musicalities of parts of the liturgy, the homiletical impulse takes over. Instead of angels and archangels, we get a hurried little exposition of their demythologized meaning. Most new orders merely turn the whole service into a rather dull and inefficient sermon—and preaching, outside the context of sacrament, prayer and praise, will be moralistic no matter how sound the intended doctrine.

IV

Music is indeed the inevitable vehicle of religion. For just this reason, *faith* can neither live with music nor without it. Given our religious fear of our own futurity, the utterance of faith will always be a sort of music against itself. When faith becomes sight, even my abstract distinction of words and music will no longer apply.

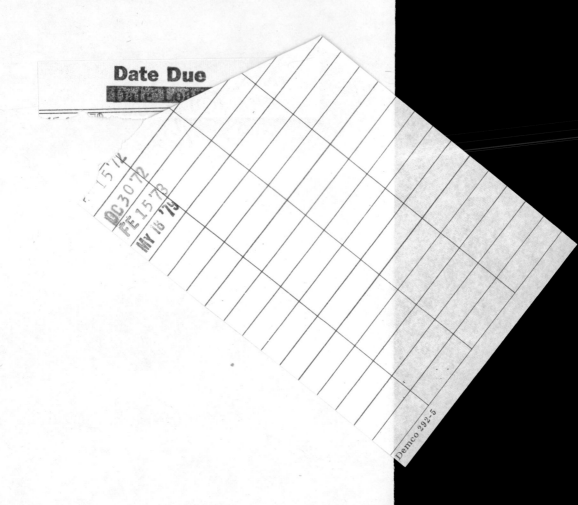